Twelve Lessons

The Journal

By Kate Spencer

Published by Katherine Spencer Publishing

Copyright © Kate Spencer, 2017
All rights reserved

ISBN: 978-1-9998613-1-5
Paperback

This book is sold subject to the condition that it shall not, by way of trade or otherwise, be lent, resold, hired out or otherwise circulated without the publisher's prior consent in any form of binding or cover other than that in which it is published and without a similar condition including this condition being imposed on the subsequent purchaser.

The scanning, uploading and distribution of this book via the internet or via any other means without the permission of the publisher is illegal and punishable by law. Please purchase only authorised electronic editions and do not participate in or encourage electronic piracy of copyrighted materials.

Your support of the author's rights is appreciated.

From My Heart to Yours

For me, the biggest lesson of the last 12 months has to be Self-Care. I admit it - I initially thought that the whole concept was a bit lame. A social media status about "me time" made my skin crawl. I wanted to write sarcastic comments all over it about getting out there and making it happen instead of just "being".

I was a warrior of the light. A leader. A voice. Here to reach as many people as I could and help them to see their magnificence. I could work around the clock and juggle a million things. People said they didn't know how I managed to fit so much in. My ego patted me on the back and applauded. And then the inevitable. I crashed, and my superhero cape stopped flying and started tying me up in knots.

In the quest for looking after others, I'd given too much of myself. The drive to support, illuminate and help heal humanity had depleted me beyond belief. The energy reserves I had left were so pitiful they hardly fuelled the essentials of my day to day life. And I was forced to learn the lesson of looking after myself.

Physical exhaustion was just the initial heads up. The brink of emotional burn out was a scary place to be, and the loss of bandwidth and capacity to function was horrifying. Epiphany moments showed me that what I was sending out to the Universe was that my time and energy were not worth protecting. And so I attracted in people and experiences that were a match to this. I had nothing much left to give and I had to withdraw. I had made myself too available, confusing this with the authenticity that I know I want to live and portray.

But I cannot be all things to all people, and neither can you. Big hearted me never wanted to turn anyone away that I could have helped. But in taking on everyone else's stuff I had stopped helping me, and the people I loved. The people who are important in my life deserve a version of me that can be present, patient, kind, funny and connected. And so do I.

I've had to be really honest with myself about what and who matters in my life, and make sure that myself and my own wellbeing are at the top of that list. I have had to assert much better boundaries and adopt a no drama policy as best I can. And above all I have had to know that this is not selfish at all, and that self-care is entirely my own responsibility, and it always will be. This experience has inspired me to write a chapter for you on something I call Tin Bucket Self Care, you'll see why when you read it.

As always, take what you need from my experience and my writing, and adapt, apply and dismiss as appropriate in your own life. My final words of wisdom on this are that the only thing that is lame about self-care, is thinking it's lame in the first place.

Love Kate x

How to Use this Book

You can read this book cover to cover, dip in and out as it suits, or ask the Universe what is right for you to know right now and then open it at random. *The Twelve Lessons Journal* has been attracted into your experience because there is a vibrational match in some way, in other words there is something in here for you that will serve your greater good, don't ignore that.

Have a belief that you are getting what is meant for you in a given moment, suspend your ego and open your heart. After you have studied some or all of the lessons, you may want to get a little woo woo and read about working with energy, rituals and the Universe.

The Monthly Manifesting process of reviewing, releasing and renewing your focus will help you to stay clear about what you want to draw into your experience, and help you to stay aligned with receiving it.

There is plenty of space to doodle, write affirmations and notes and I encourage you to. Make this journal your sounding board, your daydream and your compass. There is great value in the journey back to you.

Love Kate x

"One day or day one. You decide."

~ Paulo Coelho

www.kate-spencer.com

My gift to you...
Download your Twelve Lessons Journal audio mp3s here:
www.kate-spencer.com/twelve-lessons-journal-2018-bonuses/

Lesson 1
The Phoenix ~ Be Open to Possibility

~ A Journey of a Thousand Miles begins with a Single Step ~ Lao Tzu

This book may have landed in your lap at a time of transition, or in the middle of a regular week. But whenever it showed up, we'll call the perfect time. Because it brings with it the possibility of real change and evolution.

A word to the wise – your ego may doubt this. It could be telling you that this is the same old shizzle repackaged and sprinkled with a bit more glitter. And I don't blame it one bit for butting in. There is SO much stuff out there telling you what the formula to success is. And I'm going to say something radical here, the irony of which does not escape me. Much of it isn't going to help you. And that could include some of the content in here as well. Only what you need in any given moment. Because YOU are an authority on you. You know your story, your hopes and your dreams, and you know what makes you tick. You know what you need to heal, what you need to work on and what it feels like to walk in your shoes. You and only you.

The world has evolved in a direction where we are bombarded with information about how we need to change. The latest diet, the rules for relationships, the way to manifest a life that we love. The subtext of this information overload is that we don't know what the hell we are doing. That we need guidance from gurus, coaches and thought leaders to tell us the secret that's going to change everything. And when someone else's advice doesn't help you to feel more peace, love and happiness you feel like you are the one to blame.

We have been programmed to give away our power and not trust ourselves. I am telling you now, right from the get–go that I can't fix you. But I know someone who can. And you know them too because it's the person who you see every day in the mirror.

Now I'm not saying here that every book that's been written and every seminar you've been to hasn't been helpful. There are some great thought leaders of our time that are bringing forth some truly evolutionary insights. They may well be experts in their field, but they are not an expert on you. It's not the content that I am getting at, it's the pre-supposition that so many of us have bought into - that other people know better than we do about us. That's a harmful and powerless place for you to put your beliefs. It's not true and it can lead to guilt and shame when someone else's idea of what's going to help you ends up not helping you.

I am not blaming the authors of the books or the admin of the Facebook pages that deliver the information, hell I'm a part of the system. I don't blame you either, because we live in a world where we are bombarded with "expert advice", we feel a constant pressure to improve and keep up with what the media portrays as success. It's what we have created as a collective. But at this impasse, I ask you to pause. Choose to take back the power that you unconsciously gave away. It's time to start stepping into a new paradigm. One that is self-driven, empowered and deeply, deeply personal. A way of navigating life that brings forth your authenticity, aligns you with your truth and helps you to come out as yourself – finally. Fostering a knowing that you are perfect in your imperfection. A glorious work in progress that by far and away knows what they want and what they need to do, in order to claim the life that they came here to live.

I'm asking you from my heart - please get into yours. It's time to call you out for continually feeling like you are broken, and someone else can mend you. No one else has the missing ingredient that you need to live a life more awesome. The truth is that the only person who can truly help you is you. So what the hell have I written this book for if you've already got the answers? Because it's a framework. A collection of concepts and ideas that you may resonate with, at certain times and in situations that life brings to your door.

I believe that we all come here as souls with a curriculum of lessons that we need to learn. Unique expressions of creative consciousness wrapped up in human form. So brilliantly different to everyone else that nothing can be considered a standard fix for our lives. But I also believe that we sometimes need guidance, sign posting, encouragement and wisdom from other souls that have experienced life in their own unique way too. It's our Divine Responsibility to take that information, weigh and measure it and see what feels right to apply to our own life. This is about you trusting yourself to know what feels right and when. As with everything you will read, this book is filtered through a human mind and personality.

It's got Kate Spencer written all over it, and although its created with all of the love and intention to help support you in your life, I will not elevate myself to the position of being able to tell you what to do or how to live. YOU know best when it comes to you. Change can happen in a moment. And so it does, in every moment that we live and breathe and every moment after we stop. It's the nature of things, the ebb and the flow of existence. But what about real change? The kind of change that you dream about? The change that has the power to bring you the joy, happiness, connection and wellbeing that we all want to experience. Does that really exist? Not when you give your power away to someone else.

Lesson 1 is about being open to possibility. I am asking you here to try on the idea that you lasting and positive change can happen in your life, but only when it's self-driven and self-actualised. Many of us don't trust ourselves anymore to make the change we want. We think that we've messed up so far and we need someone to help get us out of the shit we feel like we are drowning in. What if the other person that you needed was a more empowered version of yourself? You have forgotten that you are powerful beyond belief. This has to be the first lesson. Because without you opening your mind and your heart, the rest is pointless. That door you closed and bolted on a situation, a relationship, a hope, dream or wish might be shut tight for now. But you are the one that holds the key. You can start to make shifts in your life, raise your standards and believe in yourself again. Open yourself up to the possibility that you are your own hero. Dig deep and get the hell on with it. Can you imagine a world where we all did just that? How the dots would start to join up for all of us in amazing ways? Start with yourself. Know you can do this. Take what you need and for feck's sake take action. There is a shift in consciousness occurring on our planet. And you are here, right now as a part of it. You don't get to opt out. And you came here at the right time to make a difference to you and everyone else, as yourself. The real version of yourself that only you can find.

The old ways are no longer working. We are seeing the results of human ego and greed all around us, as humanity suffers and we become more disillusioned with our so-called leaders. We may feel helpless, at the mercy of corporations that seem to rule the world in industries such as pharmaceuticals and oil. Politics is so dramatic and toxic our real life news reports could be packaged up and sold as a box set on Netflix.

There's a whole load more, of course, we could debate all day about our junk food society, the state of the education system, heath care, war, drugs, guns, racism, poverty, economic migrants and everything else that makes our heart ache. And part of that heartache is that we feel utterly helpless. I get it, I really do. You are most certainly not alone in feeling this way. Again - be open to possibility and then start with yourself. And I don't mean that in a new age mumbo jumbo kind of a way. Or in a billy-basic, lip service, so what kind of way. I am asking you now to really, really think about this as a concept.

We are ALL a part of the bigger picture here. This is not the time to be self-orientated, self-pitying or excuse making. We need everyone to step up and to be the best version of themselves. You came here to play your part, and instead, so many of us are hiding, feeling inferior, scared to death and thinking that other people can sort us out. What if enough of us decided that we were going to evolve into the people we came here to be? Can you imagine what the world would look like if we could all dig deep and make the changes that would bring the human race into a better place? What if we took responsibility, dropped our literal and metaphorical weapons, healed our wounds, forgave those who had wronged us and started to believe that we were all good enough? Can you imagine the difference in our lives? Never underestimate the power of group intention. And never underestimate your part.

The times, they are a changing, my friend. The human race is in crisis, and we can only change it if enough of us change. We are the components that make up the whole. The truly amazing gift is that by changing things for yourself, you are helping to change them for everyone else. Each one of us who raises our vibration and starts to live more consciously has a positive effect on the whole.

Lesson 1 is Be Open to Possibility. I'm asking you to believe in yourself, more than that I'm asking you to do what feels right for you and to ignore the rest.

To be open to the possibility that you can make great decisions, listen to your internal guidance system and motivate yourself to become who you came to be.

As you read on through the lessons in this book that you'll weigh and measure each one accordingly and take what you need, and only that. You might even flit back and forth and read them out of sequence. Or you could choose to ask your higher self what you need to know right now, and open the book at random. But know that you'll feel what is right, and you'll apply what you need to. And that this may well become your new default setting, as you start to trust more and empower yourself.

Welcome to the beginning of the rest of your life. This is the only place that change can start. And it's time.

How could you open your mind and heart more to the possibility there is more?

Is there a part of you that is closed to things they can't see, touch or feel?

Are you ready to entertain the thought that new experiences and perspectives could be beneficial?

"I AM open to new possibilities; I look at my world with an open mind and create miracles in every moment."

LESSON 2

Self sabotage

I AM releasing all that is not in alignment with my greatest good now. I step into the light, it is my turn to shine.

Lesson 2
Shadow Self ~ Self-Sabotage

~ It is not the mountain we conquer, but ourselves
~ Sir Edmund Hillary

There comes a time on your journey of evolution where you are ready to look within. As self-awareness grows, so does personal responsibility. We start to align with the value of finding and being our authentic self. The version of us that existed before life happened. Before we were wounded and scarred and built up our emotional armour. The armour that's sometimes so heavy we can barely see our light trying to shine through the gaps in the chainmail, around our heart and soul.

Shadow work can help you get to the root of the experiences that caused you to lockdown. It can support you to bring the parts of you that hide in the depths of your subconscious mind, into the love, light and acceptance of consciousness. A place where darkness, fear and judgment don't exist.

Once we can see from our current and more enlightened perspective how we had felt shame, guilt and judgment, it's easier to see how we abandoned a part of ourselves in order to fit into the world. Shadow work shows you the past through a lens of compassion – for yourself and The Shadow Creators in your life. We are all doing the best we can in any moment, this one included.

Your Shadow is the collection of stuff that the world has not approved of. The behaviour, traits and patterns that you've unconsciously disassociated from, so that you can be loved and accepted by others. Once banished to the subconscious it feels like they don't exist; superficially this feels good.

The truth is that these parts of us are still there, wanting to be loved and reintegrated as part of our authentic self, and they may be sabotaging our lives in different ways. Your Shadow is going to show up in contrast to who you think you are, and the version of you that you project to the world. The "F" Bomb in front of the kids. The healer who eats a diet full of processed food. The passive aggressive spouse. The school run mum who gets road rage. The well-liked manager who subtly gaslights a vulnerable colleague.

Your Shadow contains the truth of who you are in your human imperfection. The parts of you that have been judged as not good enough, that you feel shame about, and try to hide from yourself and others.

Here's a liberating thought – we ALL have this going on. Here's another one – "F" it, we ALL have this going on. Right here and right now, let yourself off the hook. You are not broken. You are a fabulous work in progress and you are doing the best with what you've got. You've got Shadow aspects, and it might just be time to look at them. No drama, no judgment.

How the Shadow Forms

We are all people pleasers, from the moment we arrive. Each and every one of us wants love and acceptance, and we want to feel worthy of fitting in. We live in a world that gives us constant feedback on how we show up. As children our parents will show us that they are approving or disapproving of what we do, if we eat until the plate is clean then this is a behaviour that makes them happy - if not, we are given feedback that this is not ok.

Feedback may be verbal or not - a lecture on the starving children all over the world, or a raised eyebrow. Regardless, it is feedback that we have "done wrong" and depending on the need we have for love and approval from that person at that time, we may well adapt our behaviour to gain it.

In this simple example we may relegate the trait we have of self-regulating our food intake to our Shadow, and disassociate from it, denying its existence in our conscious mind. Instead we start to eat more to gain the approval that comes with a clean plate. This can then become a sabotaging pattern for us, but the need for love and approval is greater at that point in time than our need to be our authentic selves. It's not until we end up at Weight Watchers as an adult, that we start to join up the dots and see this is a behaviour which does not serve us. We are likely to be unaware of where it came from and how it started.

As children especially, the need for love and acceptance is a survival instinct. We are reliant on our parents for everything and therefore mould who we becoming depending on their feedback. As feedback is repeated and reinforced, we learn to shape our behaviour based on their expectations, and then others as we are socialised. What is natural and authentic to us but attracts negative feedback from others, will often be moved into the Shadow. This creates a struggle, as the Shadow is an undercurrent of incongruence that is ever present. Because we are unaware of these aspects of self, they continue to trip us up and keep us entrenched in responses and behaviours that do not serve us, take our power away and stop us from being the whole, congruent, authentic person that we can be.

Shadow work can therefore be one of the greatest transformational and liberating tools that you will ever use. It can help you to get to the very root of an issue, and then through conscious observation and processing can help you to reintegrate the part of you that you have denied for so long. This has numerous positive effects in your life. You will feel released from reacting in a negative way that you don't understand. You'll feel more whole, connected and accepting of self, and you'll show up in your life in a way that is more aligned to who you really are in truth.

From a Law of Attraction perspective, you will be showing up as the version of you that is authentic. You'll attract people and situations that are aligned to that – and by default you will attract fewer experiences that are lined up energetically with unworthiness, hiding your true self and not feeling like you are ever going to be good enough.

The vibrational undercurrent of our Shadow is ever present until we can change the energy and meaning of our history and self, and begin to heal in the light of consciousness.

Gifts in the Shadows

The Shadow can hold some of our greatest gifts that we have repressed. Why would you ever repress and dissociate from something that's good about you? Remember that this is not intentional or a conscious act, and that it is in response to the way that other people's reactions make you feel.

If someone else feels threatened, jealous or uncomfortable with who we are and gives us that feedback in an unconscious way, this can make us feel bad. If this happens at a point in our life where we have not shored up a great deal of resilience and we are reliant on that person's acceptance and approval, we can unconsciously disassociate from talents, gifts and abilities. An example might be a music teacher who hears you sing beautifully at a young age, and they criticise and mock you in front of your classmates. At this point you want to protect your self-worth, fit in with the class and remain in approval with the teacher, so you stop singing. Fast forward thirty years and after a couple of glasses of wine one night you sing your heart out on the karaoke. You don't know why you can only let loose when you have alcohol-fuelled confidence, and generally why you hide this talent away. It feels a bit off, wrong, out of sync for some reason and you wish you could just get over it and do what makes you feel good.

Shadow work helps you to see what really played out from a conscious perspective and once you can dig deep and bring the experience into your evolved adult awareness, you find that you no longer need to hide your voice. Just because your light illuminates the wounds in others that they are not prepared to heal, does not mean that you should not shine.

The Vibration of the Shadow

When we don't work on our Shadow, we are unintentionally engaging in self-reproach. The vibrational subtext to the Universe is that there are parts of us which are not good enough to be seen and heard, a part of us is broken or unacceptable. You are not damaged, negative or an inferior human if you have a Shadow, it's a normal side effect of living a life on earth. Becoming conscious of what is held there and integrating it is a gift to yourself and others. It's brave and responsible, and it will raise your vibration with every layer you can shed, and every piece of yourself that you can bring back into consciousness.

Shadow Formation in Adulthood

The Shadow is often associated with childhood, but it's important to know that adult experiences can also influence what we unconsciously disassociate from. Any interaction that results in you receiving negative feedback from a person or group of people for your behaviour or traits can contribute to your Shadow. That includes your friends, your colleagues, your partner, or anyone else along the way. Adult examples may include being in a relationship where a partner withdraws approval when you wear clothes that make you look attractive. Depending on your own resilience, self-worth at that time and your need for approval and acceptance from them, you may find that you subconsciously start to adapt more to their expectations.

The verbal and non-verbal feedback they give you depending on what you wear will tell you whether they are approving of your choice or not, and you may find that your subconscious influences your choice of clothing based on this. You supress the part of you that wants to look feminine and sexy into your Shadow. This may surface on a girl's night out when you wear something that's considered to be "out there" because you just feel like it, you don't know why.

It's Their Stuff, Too

When we unconsciously adapt our behaviour solely because of another person's disapproval, we are giving our power away. This is different to compromise, where there is an energy of fair exchange and an intention of bringing peace for both parties. It is tempting to demonise the person who is with holding their approval or acceptance of you as being controlling, sometimes they might be.

Know that the only person that you can change is yourself, and the more conscious you become, the more empowered you can become. When you act or behave in a way that draws in disapproval from others, notice this consciously and decide that you don't have to take this on. Remember that this is their reaction. They may be looking at the world through old wounds and limiting beliefs whilst projecting onto you. It's a chance to have compassion for them and empower both of you at the same time.

The more conscious and self-aware you become, you will be more aware of the feeling that you need to adapt who you are based on other people's feedback. This means that as you are doing the Shadow work that you need to on events of the past, you will be less likely to accumulate more Shadow aspects in the now.

Prepare to Meet your Shadow

This kind of work is not for the faint-hearted, but that doesn't mean you shouldn't do it. It can bring up big stuff, but can also heal at a very fundamental level and help you hugely. Being responsible for yourself means you need to trust that you will know when the time is right to start this journey.

Some may find that an ongoing process is most helpful, and as feelings and prompts come up in their life they like to carve out space and do the work. Others may need to find some breathing space in their lives, such as taking a holiday, or time away from work, or scaling back on social activities, before they start digging deep. Do what feels right to you. Whenever and however you do this, be gentle with yourself. Commit to the process and to getting to the root of an issue, but do so with self-love and self-care in abundance. Give yourself the gift of doing it as thoroughly as you can, and know that once you start to pick at a scab you may well uncover more than you anticipated. Humans are complex creatures, and Shadow work is a journey into the unlit maze of the unconscious where you will encounter dead ends, shortcuts and interconnectedness that may come as a surprise.

For example, you may find that having a conscious look at your relationship with your colleague and why you feel so jealous (an emotion you have repressed into the Shadow but you became aware of when they were promoted over you, and you made some very loaded comments to the girl on reception, that are not like you at all...) starts to lead you towards looking at other moments in your life where this emotion has surfaced in an unconscious way and been unhelpful or harmful.

The journey back to the starting point (the moment that the trait was first repressed due to social disapproval) in itself is illuminating and may well require conscious review and healing on the way to the root of the issue that you are looking at.

As the dots start to join up, you may find journaling a helpful process as you delve deep into your Shadow and uncover emotions, behaviours and experiences that are related. Making conscious links from a now time perspective can help you to see how one repressed trait can affect different aspects of your life and relationships, therefore giving you back more of yourself and making a greater overall improvement and authenticity.

Sitting with Your Shadow

So how do you actually do Shadow work? There are lots of different ways, suggestions and methods and also books and practitioners out there which are solely dedicated to this subject. Here's my take on it.

Firstly get ready to be both honest and kind with yourself, as well as uncomfortable. Secondly set a clear intention that this is for your highest and greatest good, and that it's going to take as long as it takes but know that this isn't an excuse to get stuck in the process either. Once you have committed to the journey keep going as best you can. Trust that you'll know when you've done what you need to on a certain issue.

You may want to set a clear boundary between your Shadow work and your day to day life by using ritual, sacred space and an actual appointment with yourself. A clear definition of the pocket of time that you allocate to Shadow work can be useful. You can incorporate ritual such as lighting a candle at the outset and dedicating this to your soul's progress, and then blowing it out when the session is complete.

If you know what you want to work on specifically, set this as your intention, if not something general like bringing healing, integration and consciousness to the Shadow parts of you that are ready to be worked with can be perfect. Of course as with all therapy and personal development there will be epiphanies, realisations and feelings come up outside of your allocated slot that may need processing or consideration. Allow this to happen as best you can. If something feels heavy, upsetting or like you need to dedicate time to it, sometimes making a note in your journal and then coming back to it in a full session is useful. This acknowledges the issue and feelings that are coming up and thus stops further dissociation, but also protects your emotional and psychological wellbeing if you are in a situation where you cannot engage fully with them – such as in the middle of your working day.

You may want to have some soft or meditative music playing, a comforting warm drink in a favourite mug, a soft place to lie or sit down and a journal and pen. Once it's time to get still, to go within and to really be with yourself. Allow the feelings to come up that need to come up. If nothing comes up then ask to release resistance to the process and hand over to your Higher Self. This helps to bring a feeling of relief and gets your ego out of the way. A guided meditation can assist you if you get stuck.

Name and claim the feeling in your mind without any judgment at all. Take the role of an observer and know that all is well. Remember that whatever you are feeling or perceiving is a message to your psyche that there is work to be done. The feeling is the flag or a marker, but it's on the surface layer to mark the wound that's buried deep and needs to be brought into conscious awareness, and thus healed. Throughout our lives these unhealed, judged and disassociated aspects of self are going to keep coming up until you notice them and do the work. And if you don't do the work they will keep coming up anyway and play out in ways that hold you back and sabotage you. I say this again to give you courage to keep going and to remind you that you are doing great work.

Once you have given yourself permission to truly immerse yourself into the feeling or pattern that you are working on, it's time to journey back to the start. Ultimately, we want to be able to observe the first time that you felt this emotion or experience, this is the root of the dissociation and the moment that the Shadow aspect was created.

On your journey back to the beginning you are likely to remember other moments that you have felt this way. These may need to be processed as they come up using the steps below, and then finally applying the steps to the initial memory. Remember that we are not going through this to judge ourselves or others. As you sift through your memories and emotions, remain the observer as much as you can. From your present moment more evolved perspective, it's time to process the past in a safe, compassionate and conscious way using these three steps.

Step 1 – Gently reconnect with your past self.

Gently bring yourself back into that situation. It may help you if you engage your senses and ask yourself what you can hear, see, smell, taste and touch at this time. (Depending on how you process information you may find that you are more visual, auditory, kinaesthetic or tactile, and drawing on your senses can help you to connect to the moment more easily. Think of the way a song on the radio or the smell of sunscreen can trigger strong feelings from the past.) How do you feel and what do you perceive is happening? What was going on situationally? Who else was there? What do you observe in terms of other people's reactions? How do you react to their reaction?

Step 2 – Higher Self Perspective.

Metaphorically step back and take a helicopter view or Higher Self perspective. Become an observer of the whole situation, not just what you perceived as yourself. This is an opportunity for you to gain insight into what roles other people played in creating this Shadow aspect of yourself. What do you feel was going on for them at that time, what motivated them to give you the feedback they did or to contribute in such a way? Intend that you are able to see now what you couldn't see then, and ask if there is anything else you need to understand this.

Step 3 – How can this be healed and integrated?

Often the act of consciously observing the creation of a disassociation is enough to bring the trait, behaviour or aspect of self that has been repressed into the conscious mind, awareness and to facilitate profound healing. Compassion is usually felt for self and others, based on a core appreciation of the fact that everyone is doing the best that they can in any given moment. Being able to consciously observe and perceive someone else's standpoint and motives can release you from feelings of resentment that you may have carried and repressed for many years. You may gain an understanding that someone was trying to protect you in some way, or perhaps they were projecting their own limiting beliefs, fears or judgments. That version of them was doing the best that they could at that time, and so were you.

Once you have gone through the process, it may be helpful for you to close it off with a symbolic act or ritual. Ideas that may feel right to you could include writing a letter to those involved expressing your feelings now and from the past, and then symbolically burning it asking for all to be resolved and healed. You may also, or alternatively, want to write a letter to your former self, from a now time perspective explaining that you are doing the best you can right now, and you were then as well.

You are a Shadow Creator for Others

As you become more conscious of how Shadow aspects are created, and develop more self-awareness, you can start to see how you may have contributed to the formation of other people's Shadow. This is especially evident when you are a parent and you can see your child moulding their behaviour to fit with the approval and expectations of others around them, including yourself. Being present and being conscious is the key here, and not feeling guilty about what you may have co-created in the past.

I am a great believer in the statement, "when you know better, you do better". The more conscious we get and the more healing we can do on ourselves, the more Shadow aspects that we can integrate and the more forgiveness and compassion we can exercise, the more we change. Looking back retrospectively on who you used to be with judgment is both unproductive and unfair, your power to change is in the now. How you show up now and your willingness to heal your past is what matters. I am ok with telling my child that I might have messed up. I might have said some stuff that was coming from fear, shame, guilt or my own wounds and I could well have given them a skewed and unproductive insight or two. I am a work in progress, and it is important to let a child see that this is the case. It frees them from the notion that you must get everything right all of the time, and constantly encourages self-improvement. Through conscious conversation, apology or simply showing up and being present, I can help heal Shadow aspects in others that I may have unintentionally co-created for my child. The more evolved I become through doing my own work, the less I am likely to contribute in an unconscious way to anyone else's life or perception of themselves moving forwards.

Which recurring patterns in your life do you need to heal?

Where are you sabotaging yourself in your life?

How do you want to show up for yourself and others?

"I AM releasing all that is not in alignment with my greatest good now. I step into the light, it is my turn to shine."

LESSON 3

You attract what you are

Lesson 3
Attraction ~ You Attract What You Are

> ~ You live in a vibrational Universe, you can control the signal you emit ~ Esther Hicks

There is so much information out there about The Law of Attraction, that if you've missed it you must have been off the grid. In essence, it's a Universal Law that is rooted in the two principles that everything is made from energy, and that energy is magnetic. Everything in our physical world, including us, is made from energy, and we can work on changing the energy or vibration that we send out in order to draw in matching experiences that we want.

The Law of Attraction has become a really popular concept and tool in the modern day culture of personal development and conscious evolution. We have discovered as humans that we live in a Vibrational Universe; not only is everything energy, everything also has a frequency or a vibe and when the vibe that you send out matches what you want, life delivers it to you wrapped up in something we call manifestation. The principles are simple, but the practice of it is not easy.

Some would have you believe that it is easy, and part of the positivity movement of our time is to tell you that you can manifest the fast cars and the wealth you dream of. (There's a subtext there that this is going to make you feel better, of course, we'll get back to that at some point but hopefully you're starting to see that this is not the case.) Many of us end up not being able to draw in what we want, and we feel like a failure. This feeling like a failure then ironically sets off a vibration within you that stops the good stuff coming in for sure, and your personality and ego chip in and tell you one of two things, either this Law of Attraction stuff is a load of BS, or you can't do it. Both are damaging, not only because they close the door to you trying in the future but also because feeling like a failure sucks and will create even more of the same.

So what exactly am I saying about The Law of Attraction? It does work, and I have used it to great effect. There are lots of books you can read about this and there's a chapter coming up soon about application in your own life, but before that there's some other stuff that it's wise to know too. Sometimes it has screwed me over and made me cry. The know-it-alls in the audience right now are going – Kate Spencer it was YOU that screwed it up, not the Universe, you had resistance! Cool your jets, buddy, I agree with this in part.

My self-awareness is growing, and I am becoming more in tune with both myself and the world around me, but I still get mixed results at times. Here's my opinion. There is stuff going on in the cosmic mix that we don't yet understand. Us humans have discovered The Law of Attraction and we think that it's definitive and all encompassing. We have become closed to the fact that there may be other things going on energetically and in the Universe at large. We think this is it, and I'm standing up right now and saying that I don't think it is. And this brings me some relief. It's ok, and in fact, hugely valuable to say that we don't have it all worked out yet, and that anyone who says they do is either speaking to you from the other side or perhaps a teeny bit deluded.

Believing that we don't have it all worked out lifts the need to beat myself up when shit goes down that I would never in a million years consciously attract, ask for, manifest or draw in. Don't get me wrong this is not an excuse and it's important to be conscious enough to know the difference, but there is stuff going on in the world that I cannot for one moment accept is "attraction" because that implies that it's been asked for at some level, consciously or not.

Yes I believe in soul lessons, and I believe in souls coming here to teach us things through the contrast of their own story and experiences. I know I am not alone when I say the human part of me struggles when I see suffering. My faith is rocked when I see disease, cruelty and circumstances that just seem beyond unfair. Maybe it's the big-hearted empath in me being idealistic, but is there not an easier way to learn? The only way that I have so far been able to rationalise this in my own mind is to think of it this way.

We come to earth to grow and evolve, and therefore have to go through soul lessons. Once we are on earth and in human bodies, these lessons can be really hard, traumatic and difficult. Maybe the Universe is in some way joining up the dots on what we need for our evolution. Perhaps as humans we cannot see what we need to truly grow, and perhaps this is the Universe giving us the very best opportunity to become all that we can be. This is the nearest explanation I have at the moment, along with the Shit Happens factor.

Sometimes you can't explain what happens at all. You can pixie and unicorn it up as much as you like; it's still gonna be shit. I don't say that to be dismissive or disrespectful of anyone's beliefs or teachings. I'm not taking anything away here, I'm adding something in to consider. I say it to release me from any feelings of judgment or superiority, because when you are fixed with the opinion that The Law of Attraction is absolute, there can be a subtext of blaming others for the challenges and traumas that they experience.

That undercurrent flows with a subtle superiority when we look at the lives of others and judge them for what they are experiencing - because they created it themselves. The goes the same for us. I find relief in the fact that I am doing my best to align, allow and let the good stuff in but sometimes Shit Happens. Things go on from time to time that we just can't control or understand, and to think otherwise is arrogant and judgmental.

A diagnosis of cancer, living in a war torn country, or being the victim of a terrorist attack. None of this is "attracted" and sometimes really awful Shit Happens. The list goes on, of course, and I don't want to doom and gloom you. As evolved and conscious beings we need to rise up from the idea that this is attracted, and the subtext that it is deserved and we had a choice. Let the blaming and shaming go. Let's all get off our spiritual high horse and know that we don't know it all yet. You are a work in progress and so is our understanding of the Universe. Law of Attraction rocks - but Shit Happens. So let yourself off the cosmic hook and keep doing the best you can.

What are you attracting into your life at the moment?

What would you like to change about this?

What can you do to change your point of attraction?

"I AM attracting all things good into my life."

"May your choices reflect your hopes, not your fears."

~ Nelson Mandela

LESSON 4

Release what does not serve you

I AM releasing
what does
not serve me
now with grace
and ease.

Lesson 4
The Web ~ Old Stuff Keeps You Stuck

~ Be willing to surrender what you are for what you could become ~ Mahatma Gandhi

It sounds easy. Just let it go, release it, cut the cords and run in the opposite direction. Don't give it any thought. Stop thinking and feeling about the past and what lives there. Move forward, release what does not serve you. But as humans it's not all that easy, is it?

We hang on to stuff. That stuff might be physical, emotional, mental or spiritual.

It could be thin clothes in the wardrobe that we will slim into one day, our old story, a connection with the past that caused us harm, friendships and relationships that have long since expired, careers that we resent and situations that drain our heart and soul.

If you just sighed with recognition when you read through that list, you are not alone. This is something that we all have going on at some point in our lives to varying degrees. It's a part of the human condition that we find it hard to let go and release whatever it is that is weighing us down. It might be harmful to us, but there is a toxic comfort in familiarity and often the fear of the unknown combines with this in a cloud of stuck energy that keeps us where we know, but where we have outgrown hugely.

When you feel that something no longer serves you, the energy changes. Things become difficult and stop flowing. You get irritated and resentful. You feel drained when you are actually in a situation, exchange or place and you feel repelled before you go into it. There's a sense of doom and gloom, a heart sink or a feeling of obligation that overrides any good feelings that you used to have.

This is because the opposite of Law of Attraction is happening. It's a kind of energetic dissonance, where you are trying to push a square peg into a round hole. The feelings that you are having are the heads-up that this is not serving you, and here's a massive truth bomb – it's not serving others either, because if it was then there would be alignment from both sides.

There are two things that make releasing difficult. The first thing is that although this is likely to be in the best interests of others involved as well (if you are feeling resentment, dissonance and disconnection with people and / or situations), they may not be able to see this as clearly as you. This means that sometimes you are going to have to be the hero and be honest on everyone's behalf.

People who don't feel the mismatch as clearly as you, are likely to react. The anticipation of their reaction is often what stops us from being honest with both ourselves and them. Hold an intention that any change is for the greatest and highest good of all concerned, step back from what's happening and ask yourself if this truly serves you. (If a situation is harmful to you, you may be forced to disconnect suddenly and altogether.) Then ask what the best course of action is. You may want to get yourself into a safe and relaxed space and light a candle, play some soft music and journal out all aspects of a situation or relationship.

Ask yourself if this can evolve into something more positive and better fitting and how that might happen. Try to step back and observe rather than being yourself; this helps you to have a more objective opinion and clearer viewpoint. If there is a great amount of gravity attached to decisions around releasing situations or people in your life, then you may want to spend some time visualising the situation from their perspective and see if you can gain useful insights for evolution. Releasing what does not serve you may mean releasing an old version of a situation or relationship in order to bring positive change, or it may mean releasing it entirely.

Once your intention is set, release may be slow, like peeling off a strip of Velcro hook by hook. Or you may need to rip off the plaster that's covered a wound you've been hiding for years, in order for you to finally heal. Only you will know if it's vital to make changes immediately, and if it's not you are likely to make better decisions all round and afford yourself more relief, if you have time to weigh and measure things consciously.

Whatever feels right to you after this, is by default right for everyone. Even though others may not see or feel this straightaway, it's important to know that when you stay in a situation through obligation that you know no longer serves you, you are sending out a vibration that is aligned with "I don't matter", and this is never true. It's a harsh observation, but how other people react is their responsibility. Of course have love and compassion in your heart, and everyone's best interests held tight in your overall intention, but know too that we each choose how we react and behave. It is often the fear of another person's reaction that makes us give up on ourselves. What if by you staying in a situation that did not serve you, you were robbing another soul of becoming who they could be too?

This is not me saying you should leave a relationship or to walk out on your job. It's simply a wake-up call that I am offering to you in order for you to have an honest life audit and see what no longer fits, what may need to evolve and how you can live more of your truth. This is not a selfish process, it's an evolved and conscious way of living and it's ongoing.

Physical Release

Sometimes what does not serve us is an accumulation of physical stuff that we've gathered throughout our life to date. Clutter is the collective word for these items, and when your life is full of it, your vibration can be affected in a detrimental way. Emotional overwhelm can result as well as frustration if you can't find what you need to in a cluttered environment. Energetic "noise" can be an issue, especially if you are energy sensitive, because everything has its own frequency or vibration and many combine in one space to give you the energetic equivalent of a radio turned up loud but not tuned in properly. Combined with this are frequencies such as light, sound, earth energy, electromagnetic energy, other people's energy and your own.

On top of clutter these additional vibrations can end up making you feel bombarded, emotionally distressed and in some cases, physically ill. Compare this feeling to the feeling you get when you first walk into a hotel room that is minimally furnished, clean and clear. When you do this it's easy to make the comparison. It's not only the energy and physical existence of the stuff that you need to release that can have a negative or detrimental impact on you, it's the association that you give it too.

What have you made those "thin" clothes mean? Ask yourself what the feeling is that you experience when you see them hanging up, ready for the day that you have shed the pounds you need to in order to wear them. Do you feel motivated to eat better and exercise and head for your goal, or do you feel like a failure because they've been there for way too long and those days are gone? If items are triggering a negative feeling, emotion or association then it's time to let them go. Remember – you attract what you are.

So what good is it looking at something every day that sets up a vibrational pattern of "I am a failure". My advice is to give these clothes to a charity shop or friend and set yourself free from the old energy. This will lift and change your vibration immediately because you are helping others and living more in The Flow, and by feeling better you will start to attract better experiences to you. Have a good look around your life at the physical stuff that you have been hanging on to and check in with the way it makes you feel.

If you don't feel good then it's time to sell it, pass it on or throw it away. If you have resistance to this it's likely to be fear. Fear might come dressed up as an excuse such as not having enough time to do this, or that you need to hang on to something just in case. In truth it's the fear of letting the past go, fear that you spent so much money on stuff you are not going to use, fear that you might be able to finally breathe and become a better version of yourself.

Fear that you can't heal the wounds that you piled the clutter on top of to try to hide. Fear that you aren't good enough without all of your stuff. Sit with this and see if any of these resonate with you, or something different that's fear-related. Ask yourself what you need to make some progress and get out of fear.

Perhaps you need a friend to help you, choose someone conscious and non-judgmental that you feel safe with. Maybe you feel like you need permission – you can have mine if that helps. Focus on helping you and helping other people, and break down the task to one thing at a time. A drawer, a cupboard, a handbag. Set a timer, get some upbeat music on and have a focused fifteen minutes. You are worthy of releasing what does not serve you, and once you have made some progress you will feel accomplished and want to carry on.

Your Old Story

Releasing who you used to be can be incredibly liberating. Our "story" is the collection of beliefs that we have about ourselves, based on who were and what we have been through. Sometimes this can be empowering, and sometimes it can be disempowering, and this is based on the power of perspective. People who make the best of everything are a joy to be around, and of course the opposite is true. Have you ever asked anyone the general question of "how are you" and then ten minutes into their doom and gloom story regretted it? Everyone has had things happen to them that were a challenge, hardship, trauma or let's be honest, life kicking the shit out of them. And everyone's stuff is big stuff to them.

The important thing to know about your story is that you can look back over your life and choose what it means to you. When you exercise this power of choice you can change how you feel in the present, and the way you feel in the present is important for two reasons. First of all it's simply better to feel good rather than feel negative emotions such as hate, anger and resentment. Secondly, the way that you feel is vibrational and sends out a frequency which is matched up with experiences through The Law of Attraction. Our story and its meaning create the framework of who we are, and as such, carry a strong and dominant vibration.

When your story is based around hardship and pain, you'll find it really hard to feel positive in the present and show up in a way that's any different to that. This will have an effect on your life and relationships, and also what you draw in energetically.

The process of reframing can be useful in terms of releasing now time perceptions that you may have of your history, in other words not changing what happened but changing what it means now. Your power is in the present moment and although you cannot change what happened, you can change what you feel that it means. A simple reframing exercise is to listen to your internal dialogue about something that happened in your past. In a safe space and when you have time, reflect on something from your history that you know you still carry negative emotions about. Don't judge what you are saying to yourself, just allow it to flow for a moment. Pick out key words, phrases and feelings. These are the clues to your story about this event or situation.

You may want to note these down in your journal as you start to unpick and reframe. The things that are coming up for you are based on the way that you are looking at things. They are a representation of what you believe to be true, and where you are sending your energy. Sometimes as humans our view can be narrow and fixed, this is an opportunity for you to be more flexible and willing to see the bigger picture of your past.

Go back to the event in question as an observer in your mind's eye. Ask yourself to look for what you may not have seen before - new information brings new perspectives. Also ask yourself from your present moment viewpoint what there is to be grateful about, even something small can be built on in a positive way. Once you have that one thing, look for more. Keep looking until you have seen things in as different and positive a way as possible. Have a break and change your environment, go for a short walk, have a shower, call a friend, eat a snack. Then revisit the event in question and see if your self-talk has changed into a more positive account and therefore more positive feeling.

What are you hanging on to that you need to release?

Why are you hanging on to this?

What would your life look and feel like if you could set yourself free and let go?

"I AM releasing what does not serve me now with grace and ease."

"You get in life what you have the courage to ask for."

~ Oprah Winfrey

LESSON 5

You are a creator

I AM *consciously creating a magnificent life experience for myself now.*

Lesson 5
Universal Magic ~ You Are a Creator

~ Life is not happening to you, it's responding to you ~ Rhonda Byrne

I said earlier that I believe in The Law of Attraction, and that I have used it to great effect in my life and business. I think as long as we take into account the Shit Happens factor and get out of our human ego that thinks we know everything that's happening in the Universe all of the time, then we can get our head and heart around something that can make massive positive changes for us. As you already know, this Universal Law is rooted in the two principles that everything is made from energy, and that energy is magnetic.

We are all made up from frequency, and our frequency or vibration is entirely unique. Think of it as an energetic fingerprint that is you and you alone. The Universe is responding to the thoughts, feelings, emotions and energies that you are radiating (intentionally or not) and drawing in the experience that we call Life. This means that You Are a Creator of your life thought by thought, feeling by feeling and moment by moment. The good news is that once you become conscious of what you are sending out there, you can deliberately change it, in order to draw in more experiences that you want and less of what you don't. This is working with The Law of Attraction, Cosmic Ordering, Deliberate Creation or Co-

Creation. So how the feck do you do that? You have to work on sending out the vibration that matches up with the experience that you want to draw in – as if it's happening right now. Here are the nuts and bolts as I see it.

Be Present

In order to draw something into your life, you need to send out that matching vibration in the present moment - as if it is happening now. Therefore, all aspects of your multidimensional-self need to be grounded in the here and now time. Becoming really aware of what is going on in your environment can help you to be present, slow yourself down and look around you. Engage all of your senses, you may find that one is more dominant than the others, depending on how you process information. Then visualise sending roots down to the earth and asking to be anchored. Call to all parts of you to be in the now time including any consciousness and soul extensions. Click your fingers all around your aura and affirm "I AM here." Essential oil of Basil is very good for being in the present moment, and haematite is probably my favourite crystal for getting grounded, I usually have some in my pocket.

Activate the Vibration

In other words, you need to feel what it's going to feel like when this happens for you. Visualising your outcome through daydreaming, self-hypnosis or guided meditation can be extremely helpful. If you find that your mind comes up with resistance and your ego starts to butt in, you can always ask "What would it feel like if…" This helps the human mind and ego to cope with the incongruence of you telling yourself something has happened in order to trigger the feeling, when it hasn't actually happened yet. Allow yourself to see, hear and feel your intention unfolding in your mind's eye, your heart and your physical body. Once you have really been able to turn the feeling up as much as possible, it's sometimes a good idea to connect a relevant affirmation with the feeling, and perhaps also a physical anchor point that you can use together as triggers to help you get back into the feeling more easily in future. Examples of this might include you squeezing together your thumb and index finger into a loop or pressing the tip of your tongue behind your teeth whilst thinking your affirmation. Always think about 3Ps when creating affirmations – Positive, Present and Powerful.

Starting with I AM anchors you in the now time and makes the affirmation present tense, and then choose positive and powerful language to help activate the feeling you want.

Heal Your Wounds to Release Resistance

Old, unresolved feelings have a vibration. Every time you felt unworthy, embarrassed, or anything else hurtful or traumatic you need to do what you can to heal this. Old wounds may only show on the surface as a scar, but they could run deep and will still carry the energy of the past if they are not brought into the light and healed. You might feel ok and then find that someone happens to pick at a scab, making you feel exposed, vulnerable or reactive. More than that, though, these wounds are all a part of your core signature vibration, and they are likely to be very different to what you are trying to draw into your life.

Although you are not doing it deliberately, you are radiating out the energy in these wounds until they are healed. This is possibly the resistance that has made you feel unworthy and the opposing vibration has contributed to self-sabotage with The Law of Attraction. "Raising your vibration" in part will involve healing these old wounds and being able to move on. Otherwise you'll forever be stuck in the past and be unable to create a future you love. If you know what it is that's keeping you stuck then get to work on it, and if not, then do some work on finding out what it is. And a note on healing - smart people get help when they need it. Find out who or what works for you and get busy on healing your past in order to create your future.

Line Up & Live It

It's no good "doing" The Law of Attraction, you have to live it as much as possible. You are sending out a frequency all of the time and the Universe is responding all of the time, you can't switch it on and off. This means that as much as possible in your life you need to line up to what it is that you are creating, and the essence of that. It's no good, for instance, asking the Universe for someone to love you and you not loving yourself. Or manifesting abundance whilst feeling resentful when you pay your bills and coming from an energy of lack.

Inspired Action

Herein lies one of the points I was making about us not knowing everything about how The Law of Attraction works. I believe that in the background of life, the Universe is joining up the dots on our behalf, according to what we are sending out as frequency, what lessons we've got coming up and what's right from a Higher Self and soul evolution perspective. (With a sprinkling of Shit Happens for good measure.) Now and then you will feel like taking Inspired Action in a certain direction. You'll notice a subtle gut feeling or knowing, and you'll find that you start to follow that more and take action as opportunity comes your way.

Opportunity can sometimes be a stepping stone that's going to help you move towards your goal, or line someone or something up that will become helpful or necessary for you to progress. Remember that sometimes a detour is really a shortcut you are unaware of. If you are holding an over-arching intention that you are supported and that all is well, then it makes it easier to tune into these moments and take the action that you need to. Sometimes what we feel may be a small and unrelated action could end up opening doors that will lead us in the perfect direction.

Vision Boards

These can be a useful tool for us when working with The Law of Attraction, but they can also be a sticking point that stops you making progress. The main point I would make is that it depends on what feelings your vision board triggers within you. If you look at it and your heart sinks because you feel like you are never going to be able to create a life like the one that's shining down from your wall, then this is not helpful. If on the other hand it makes you feel excited, happy and grateful that the experiences you see are on their way to you and you want to give thanks in advance, then it's a great idea. Remember that the way you feel is the significant part of The Law of Attraction, and you want to generate good feelings in order to allow the good experiences to flow to you.

When looking at something makes us feel that we are a bit of a failure, no matter how many affirmations we say, we are sending out a vibration that will sabotage us. This is when something called Paradoxical Intent is likely to play out. It happens when you THINK that you are manifesting what you want by saying affirmations, and looking at your vision board but in reality your ego and personality are mainly feel the lack of what you want. You think you are working with The Law of Attraction effectively and get frustrated that things are not lining up for you and coming in. But what you have missed is that the vibration you're sending out is actually one of resistance because of the dominant feeling of lack. For example, let's say I really want a new car. I start saying loads of affirmations about my fabulous new car, and I stick up a picture on my vision board of the one I really want. I see this every day and keep affirming, but all this does is trigger a feeling within me that it hasn't manifested yet so I must be a failure. I am, however, committed to drawing this in, so I keep going – but nothing changes because my dominant vibration is one of lack or that I am not a success and it's not happening. For many of us this then becomes something of a cosmic irony. In our human mind and ego we think that we are manifesting, but instead we are reinforcing the feeling that it's not there, and the Universe lines up with this feeling or vibration.

When you set out to manifest something it is important that you ask for something that is Vibrationally Accessible to you. You have to be able to generate the feeling that it's happening, and therefore the vibration in order to draw it in, and sometimes the gap between where you are now and what you want is so vast that you cannot generate that feeling successfully. You then run the risk of feeling the gap more than you feel the outcome you desire and manifesting more gap, thus keeping your desires unintentionally out of reach. Adopting a step by step approach with a Vision Book can help you to stay aligned vibrationally. You still have your big goals and dreams, but by doing it this way you can get rid of the gap that swallows us up and makes us feel like a failure. Any notebook will do – I like a spiral bound one because I feel right from the get go I can be a work in progress and tear pages out if I want to!

Start at the back of the book

Write the new story of how you want your life to look in the present tense. Really go to town and write your hopes, dreams, desires and goals as if they are happening right now. Engage all of your senses, include pictures you've cut out of magazines and anything else that you want to which represents what you are creating. Remember that I AM affirmations are incredibly powerful and will not only ensure that you stay in the present, they are also a cosmic command, so it's a really great way to start a sentence in your new story. Now start to think about closing the gap between where you are now and the life you are manifesting. If I suggested to you that getting there was going to take a series of steps, what would those steps be? Think for a moment of how you would chunk down the journey between now and then, what could you set as mini goals or stepping stones to move you towards your new story? These are the steps you need to be vibrationally accessible when their turn comes.

In other words, the first step needs to be something that you can start to align with and feel at the outset of your journey. When I started to build my business I had a goal of where I wanted to be in years to come, but it felt so huge that it was nearly impossible to align with back then. I knew, however, that I could start to feel what it would feel like for me to reach fifty people in my Life & Soul Academy, and help them to change their lives. So this became my first goal, and once it was reached I started to get into the feeling place that I could reach one hundred people. Once you know what your first step is, write it down at the beginning of your book as if it's happening now. Include doodles, pictures and anything else that makes you feel happy and in alignment. Refer regularly to this and take the inspired action that comes into your awareness, put into practice all of the other aspects such as being present, keeping your vibe high, and visualising the outcome as if it's happening now and so on.

Once you have achieved your first step you can turn the page and write the next one, each time getting closer to your ultimate goal and each time staying in alignment. Metaphorically and vibrationally you are carrying around your end goal at the back of your Vision Book so the intention is always there that this is going to manifest at the perfect time. You haven't given up on it, you've just made it a whole lot easier for yourself by closing the gap.

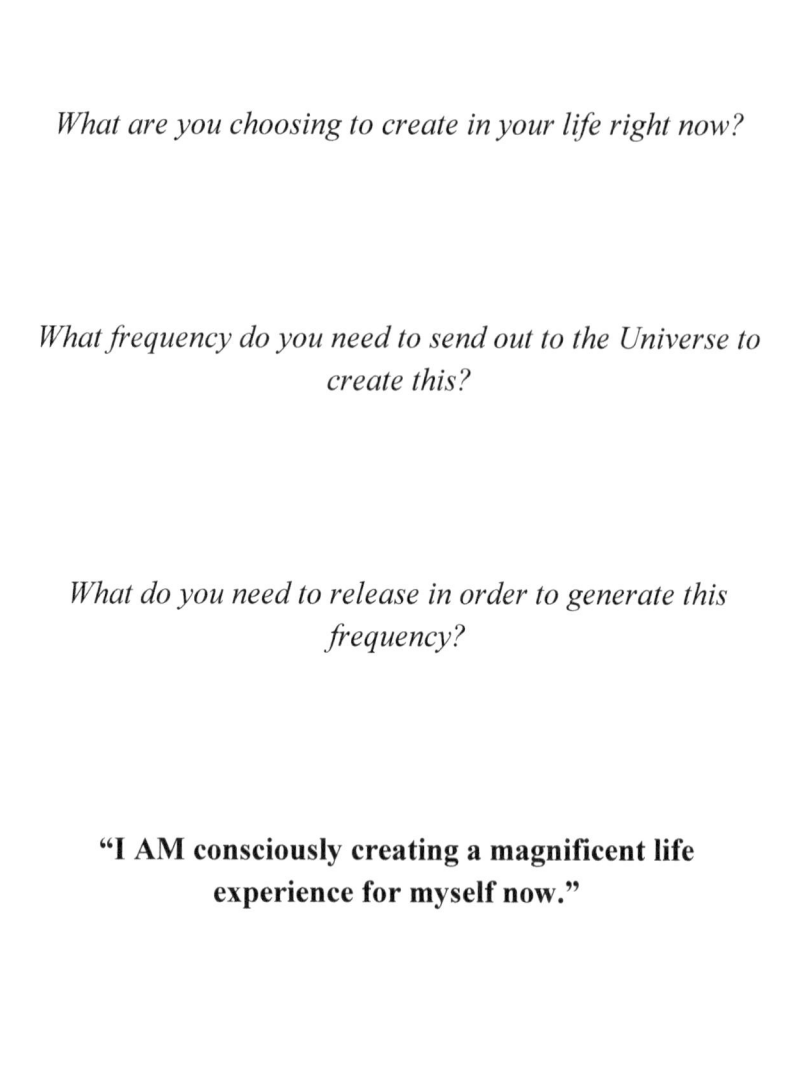

What are you choosing to create in your life right now?

What frequency do you need to send out to the Universe to create this?

What do you need to release in order to generate this frequency?

"I AM consciously creating a magnificent life experience for myself now."

LESSON 6

The law of karma

I AM releasing all vows, oaths, contracts, binds and agreements that are karmic in nature that I am ready to resolve now.

Lesson 6
The Law of Karma ~ Cause & Effect

~ There are the waves and there is the wind, seen and unseen forces. Everyone has these same elements in their lives, the seen and the unseen, karma and free will ~ Kuan Yin

Karma is usually a word that's thrown around in our human world as a concept when something goes wrong in our life, or when we want some kind of payback to happen to someone who has wronged us. Karma is a law of Cause and Effect. It's the coming back to you of what you have sent out, but unlike The Law of Attraction it is further reaching and spans across lifetimes and incarnations.

My first real insight into Karma came while I was working towards becoming a hypnotherapist and I studied spiritual regression (as an extension of my initial past life regression training). I believe in past lives and reincarnation, but this is one of those moments that I mentioned at the outset that you need to take only what works for you.

During my training I went through the process of a spiritual regression myself. The difference between this and past life regression is that you actually get to go back to the time before you were born. Some of us call this heaven, the in between or home. This is where I gained first hand insights into my soul and the vastness of the world of spirit and energy. It was beyond mind blowing, and being in an energy of everything helped me to be able to see how our human lives were a learning experience in the physical but our soul was eternal.

After being regressed down to a very young age and then my earliest childhood memory, I was taken back into the womb where I was asked questions about my soul purpose in this lifetime and why I had chosen my earth family. Some information came through that was surprising to me at that point, when I was asked how I felt I told the therapist that I was "fed up". This seemed a strange thing to say as I was preparing to be born and start my journey on earth, but when I told my mother about this she verified that she'd been on full bed rest for weeks and that she was feeling this way too. She also confirmed that I was her second child – previously her and my father hadn't spoken about the baby that had been miscarried before I was conceived.

I was then guided to take the journey back home, and I felt a pulling feeling away from the earth and my physical baby body. It took me through layers of energy that felt different. I now presume that these were dimensional in nature and before long I was orientated in a space that felt safe and familiar. A being approached me and I knew instinctively that this was my guide, and we spent some time communicating about my life to date.

I then went on to visit The Library, or what we have come to call on earth the Akashic Records. This is a vibrational record of every thought, word, deed and intention of every soul across every incarnation. It appeared to me in regression as a huge library, and this is the case for most people. This could be because of cultural expectations and the fact that this concept of a library is now a part of the collective consciousness, and also that our human mind finds the nearest representation of something intangible to help our understanding.

I was able to find my own soul records on one of the shelves; they appeared to me as a huge white book with gold lettering on the cover. As I opened the book the images inside were moving and I found that I could step into them and re-experience moments from this earth life that had passed, or even moments between lives and of past lives. I also got to meet with my Council of Elders; a group of very wise and revered old souls who oversee your progress across lifetimes and incarnations, and can help you understand more about your purpose, as well as what has gone before and what's to come in the future.

The final place I visited was The Life and Body Selection Room, which is exactly as it sounds. This room was like something from the deck of a spaceship and it had a large screen split into three sections ahead of me, and a kind of dashboard on the deck. There were three glass "pods" that showed the bodies which were under consideration for this incarnation, two were female and one was male. I was able to request that I tried on any or all of the bodies in order to see which one I felt most comfortable in, my guide was still with me and spoke about the importance of vibrational matching as well as physical form. I could then ask to see clips or snippets from the lifetimes that each body would live, and these were shown on the screen in front of me. I was told that these would be deliberately very generic to give an overall flavour or impression, but would not include detail that would influence hugely or would show future lessons that may be pre-arranged.

All in all the experience was fascinating. I want to say that as someone who holds a degree in psychology, I am aware that this could be my vivid imagination, or that I could have been led by the language that the therapist had used, any pre-suppositions that had been planted in my mind or some kind of trick. However this regression took place at the end of a week-long intensive course of study, and was performed on me as part of someone's final assessment.

It was conducted under the scrutiny of an examiner, and the criteria for admission to the course in the first place was stringent. Content had included a great deal of time talking about being very careful and conscious not to lead the client, integrity was essential throughout. Personally, I am convinced that this was a genuine experience, and one that was incredibly life affirming. It gave me great insight into myself and how I might fit in overall on earth at this time. So what has this got to do with Karma?

I went on to gain my qualification and then work with other people who wanted this kind of therapy, and although I don't do it now, it was very rewarding and interesting work to say the least. As a result of my own experience and from working with others, I do believe that each incarnation (either on earth or not, and yes I have regressed clients back to lives in other places) imprints your soul or blueprint with an energetic memory. I have helped and supported people who have had physical symptoms in this lifetime, emotional responses, fears and phobias or relationship issues, to release and heal the cause of these through their past lives, and create massive change in their current life.

Under hypnosis they describe how they have often chosen to incarnate with the same souls again, as part of a soul group to resolve Karma and pay back Karmic Debts that were created in other times and places. These members of your soul group usually represent friends and family or key people in your life.

Perhaps The Law of Karma can often highlight why we experience such dramatic life lessons and challenges in close relationships at times. It's important to add that you cannot 'clear' Karma unless someone has worked through it and understood the underlying lesson and reason behind it. Karma can be quick and come back to you almost immediately, or it can take weeks, years or lifetimes. Sometimes it is necessary to go back to the initial experience or incident, either with the help of a practitioner or yourself in a meditation or reflective state, and to consciously look at the lesson in order to release it.

You can find there is some sort of specific action you need to take. For example, breaking a vow or agreement (is this simply a focused intention to release the past from a now time perspective that changes the vibration and meaning?) exercising forgiveness or offering an apology. In my experience, no thought, action, word or deed goes unnoticed, ever. The returning of your Karma may not be an exact replica of the energy you sent out there in the first place, but there is always an association with the essence. For example, if you are a person who pokes fun at other people and has a critical attitude you may find that the Universe interprets this as you taking away the self-confidence of others. In terms of Karma you may find there is an incident of random identity fraud that means money is stolen from your back account. This is the Universe taking from you and also affecting your worth, and therein lies the association.

Each example is completely individual, so therefore trust your own intuition and gut feeling about what is playing out in your own life. It is being framed up this way so that you can recognise the lessons and grow. Interpretation is as individual as the lesson itself, so if you do seek guidance from a practitioner, make sure that you only take what resonates with you. We must all remember that even the best psychics, readers and healers are here in a human body, and as such they are filtering information through their own brain, belief system, ego and personality. So if they say something that you feel in your own intuition is not right for you, then empower yourself and don't take this on board.

Past Life or Spiritual Regression can be very useful because this process will help you to channel the information that you need when in an altered state, so it will come directly from your higher self and will not be filtered through someone else. A skilled practitioner will not lead you with their questioning and will facilitate (but not influence) what you are receiving. Karma can be released this way. Another important thing to note about Karma is that it repeats until it is resolved. If you have a Karmic Lesson coming up in your life, you will find it manifests in different guises over and over until you recognise the essence of the lesson or experience that you need to learn, resolve and release. It's often a clue in your life that you have something Karmic playing out when you keep drawing in situations and people that bring the same type of challenge. Even though you have worked on your energy and consciousness to change your resonance to these, you may find that they are still attracted into your life because the Karmic is not resolved.

You may find that you keep experiencing a circumstance or type of person over and over again and you don't know why things seem to keep turning out the same way, even though there are different players on the stage and there is a different setting. This is another clue for you that there could be Karma involved. You may find that through your meditation, intuition or work with a practitioner you have made vows and agreements in past lives that are still active in this life.

An example would be if you have been married before and vowed and promised yourself to one person, and then find that this overshadows your current life relationship, or perhaps you have taken vows of poverty as part of a religion or spiritual ceremony. These really can have a knock-on effect in your life now, and once they have been identified on a conscious level and the time comes to release them you can use this affirmation: "By divine decree and in the name of my God Presence I AM, I now break any and all vows, oaths, covenants, agreements, contracts and binds in relation to *(insert name or situation)* that I am ready to release from my consciousness, energy body, cell memories and records now."

Hold the intention that you are asking for a dispensation because you have learned what is it that you needed to experience, and that you are in gratitude for this and also for the release and resolution. You may need to use the affirmation several times if the Karma is multi-faceted, and change the wording each time. For example, this could be about a relationship breakdown but might also affect finances and your self-confidence. The Law of Karma can also return goodness into your life that you have sent out in the past, it doesn't all have to be challenging or negative. And the good thing about this is that when you live consciously you can look for opportunities to practice kindness, gratitude, forgiveness, grace and much more, that will help towards your future karma in either this life or the next.

Be mindful of the concept of Cause and Effect, and start banking good Karma that will be returned when the time is right. Because of the ascension of the earth and what is termed "The Golden Age" or "The Age of Light", many of us have incarnated at this time in order to clear lifetimes of Karma so that we can all individually contribute to the collective raising of consciousness of humanity. This means that if you are awake to your spiritual path and you have set an intention that you want to evolve, that this intention is likely to bring up more Karma and lessons for you to help you. Combine this with the soul contracts we have and the intention to help others via our own growth, this can make for a bumpy ride in our human lives right now.

Hold that things are unfolding as they should be for your highest and greatest good. Remember that you can only do the best with what you've got, at any point on the journey, and for any person this is always the truth. And remember that you are precious, a part of the Divine Plan and that All is Well.

What are the repeating lessons and experiences in your life that you feel could be karmic?

What do you need to work on, learn or release in order to resolve this?

How can you go about generating more good karma for yourself in this lifetime?

"I AM releasing all vows, contracts, oaths, contracts, binds and agreements that are karmic in nature that I am ready to resolve now."

LESSON 7

The law of reflection

I AM embracing the reflections that life is bringing me and in gratitude for the opportunity to grow.

Lesson 7
Mirror, Mirror ~ The Law of Reflection

~ The good we find in others, is in you too. The faults you find in others are your faults as well. After all to recognise something you must know it
~ Unknown

The Law of Reflection states that life is a mirror and literally reflects back to us a version of ourself. Sometimes reflections are subtle and sometimes they are blatantly obvious. This can depend on lots of things, such as how badly the Universe wants to bring the reflection to your attention for your growth and development, and also perhaps how many times you have missed the reflection in the past.

If you believe in The Law of Attraction then you believe that we draw in experiences based on what we are sending out. I believe that reflection is just that. If you've got something going on within you then you're going to be carrying a vibe that is in accordance with that in some way. This vibe then combines with everything else that is you and gets sent out there into the world at large, making up part of the frequency that is you and draws in what's a match. This can be very useful for your evolution, development and consciousness.

Progress, of course, relies on your ability to take responsibility and get out of ego, something that some of us are not good at yet. Remember that you are a work in progress and so is everyone else. None of us are perfect and self-judgment is both harmful and unhelpful at the same time. I like to see reflections as little red flags that are showing me where I am and what I need to work on. They come up in situations as reminders of who we are becoming, and sometimes as contrast for who we don't want to be. Sometimes they surface as emotional triggers, which can make us feel uncomfortable, upset, angry or irritated with a person or situation. When you feel this way, take a step back and ask yourself what The Law of Reflection wants you to see. If what you have experienced is especially ugly you may find that you need some distance from the event in order to find a clearer and less emotionally charged space to reflect back from.

It's often helpful to see your life as a play being staged on the earth. See each person in your circle (and beyond) as an actor that has a part to play in helping you to grow spiritually and personally. This way you can start to be in gratitude for reflections and not get tied up in anger, resentment, judgment or a lack of personal responsibility. Our greatest teachers bring us the most challenging reflections, and once we can be honest with ourselves and uncover what it is we need to work on (the aspect of us that has attracted this in, or the unhealed wound, limiting belief or shadow aspect), there can be very significant transformation.

It is, of course, far easier to ignore this and instead blame others for not being enlightened or awake, and unconscious people tend to do just that. Remember that we are all doing the best that we can with what we've got, and don't judge. When you are ready to work with reflections you will find that although challenging at times, the gift of growth and self-realisation that you receive is definitely worth it. The traits and examples that The Law of Reflection brings you will show you an aspect of your own consciousness to a lesser or greater degree. There may not be a literal translation here, so look for the essence that is being highlighted to you, this may take some time and introspection. You will need to be open and use your intuition to see what each reflection means to you, and how it serves you in a given moment.

Start to view reflections as gifts, and the harder they are to swallow, the greater the gift and the greater the shortcut to your own development and enlightenment. Once you are consciously aware that reflections are occurring in your life, you will become more tuned into them and feel the difference between a reflection and a random day to day occurrence. It would be contaminating, draining and tiring to go through every day of your life reading 'the reflections' into every single interaction and event. Instead, know that you are open to working with this and notice what the Universe brings to your attention. Know that when something comes on to your radar and makes you think, pricks your conscience or brings an emotional response that this is something to possibly look deeper into. Step back from this and pause for a moment, and ask for the essence of the reflection. It might come to you as a thought, feeling, knowing or realisation, or you may need to get some distance and meditate on this.

Once you have the reflection it's time for you to take an honest look at the patterns and beliefs, relationships, behaviour and traits that do not serve you and how the reflection matches up. Now you are conscious of this, you need to do your own inner work to change and evolve. You will know if the changes that you have made have been effective, because the Universe no longer needs to highlight this information to you. Reflections of this nature will stop or wane and you will no longer attract the same people and situations. Once the pattern has gone there will no longer be resonance, and nothing to bring to your attention through The Law of Reflection.

Cosmic Scab Picking is something that I believe can happen when working with reflections. This is the Universe using red flag reflections to draw your attention to some healing that needs to be done. When we are conscious enough to be able to look at reflections this way, we can find that when we are shown things that make us feel uncomfortable (and I liken this to a scab being picked at), it's sometimes because we know deep down that there is work to be done here. We may have tried to hide a wound or a trauma or disguise it in some way, but until it's healed it's still there under the façade. A reflection can come your way and pick at the top layer, in an attempt to expose what needs to be seen, processed and brought into the light of healing. We usually resist this because we are in fear, and I'm not going to say it's easy to get down and dirty with your wounds, but you know the drill. It's necessary, it's a gift and it's going to set you free.

Hold the intention that everything comes up at the perfect time. Know that you have within you whatever you need to work on it and heal it when it does come up, after all you're bound to if the time is perfect, right? This is not only encouraging, it will also bring you relief and help you to stop judging yourself about why you haven't looked at this sooner. Give thanks for the red flags, the scab picking and the actors. They are helping us to make more progress than we know, when we are prepared to see them as the catalyst that they truly are for our evolution.

What reflections are you seeing in others that make you feel irritated, uncomfortable and upset?

Which repeating reflections have you been given by different people and situations?

Which thought, feeling or behaviour pattern do you need to release in order to stop attracting these reflections?

"I AM embracing the reflections that life is bringing me and in gratitude for the opportunity to grow."

LESSON 8

Compassion and forgiveness

I AM walking free from my history. I forgive myself and others and release past hurt and trauma now. I love myself enough to free myself.

Lesson 8
Forgiveness & Compassion

~ Forgiveness is the fragrance that the violet sheds on the heel that has crushed it ~ Mark Twain

Forgiveness is an active process. It's not something that just magically happens over time, you need to be a willing spirit and an active participant to allow forgiveness, and you need to choose it for yourself. By keeping yourself bound to anger, resentment and hurt in the past you are chaining only you and not those people or situations that you feel wronged by. Forgiveness is also something that you do for yourself, not the other person or people involved. It's an act of great self-love and does not mean you are letting anyone off the hook or saying that what happened was ok. In forgiving you are saying that it's time to move forwards and time to stop allowing this to contaminate the quality of your life and relationships now and in the future.

Many of us have had experiences in our past where we have suffered in some way, physically, emotionally, financially, mentally or otherwise. These experiences can leave deep and lasting scars within us and fuel feelings of anger and pain for a long time after the initial event, and sometimes even a lifetime. As humans there is a tendency sometimes to slip into victim mode and gain some sort of satisfaction from rehashing the story of events, telling people how you were hard done by. I'm not judging you for this, it's something we are usually unaware of. When you are living consciously however, it's important to see that your ego is, at times, thriving on this, but that in truth you are stuck in a pattern that is holding you back and creating resistance in your life. I am not being harsh or uncaring when I say this, God knows my life has not been a bed of roses and I have had plenty of opportunity to practice this, and there might be more coming up! By going over the story and holding on to the anger and resentment you are keeping active the feelings and vibrations in your energy system. This can lead to physical symptoms in your body and disease over the long term, and it makes you show up in your life in a way that does not serve you. It stops you from being in the allowing space that lets energy flow easily into your life to bring you goodness and joy, and it stops you from being a nice person to be around.

When you get stuck in negative emotions such as hate and resentment, the vibrational subtext of this to the Universe is one of "I AM a Victim". When you radiate that as part of your dominant vibration, you are going to get served up with more of the same from The Law of Attraction. This will confirm to your ego that, yes indeed, you are a victim, and that life dealt you a really bad hand this time round. The life of your dreams will be kept totally out of your reach and you will contaminate relationships, opportunities and experiences time after time. This is self-sabotage in action. I know that there will be people reading this right now who think I don't understand just how bad they have had it. If that is the case then hear this – it's over, it's in the past and it's done now. You cannot change what has happened. Yes it may have been monumentally unfair and traumatic for you or yours. But there comes a time when hanging on to that is only harming one person, and that's you.

There have also been times in my life that I have really struggled and my victim mode has firmly kicked in. I wanted to rant and rave and hold on to fury as some egotistical justification that surged through me. I have wanted revenge, I have wanted to be there when the Universe served up a dish from the Karma Café to someone who had hurt me. Like you, I am a work in progress. And luckily I got to a point in my life where I could see that this attitude was harming me greatly and stopping me from making progress. The people who had hurt me in the past weren't holding me hostage in the now – I was, and I deserved better.

Here's something that your ego may not be ready to hear yet, every single person is doing the best that they can in any given moment. Some people are awake to living consciously and some are not. We have all had different childhoods, parental input (or not), incomes, siblings, schooling, interactions, experiences and histories. Each one of us has been programmed differently by our environment, our culture and those around us. The beliefs that we formed were influenced by what we saw demonstrated, what we were taught and how behaviour was rewarded or discouraged. Empathy and emotional intelligence may have been traits we established (or not), as well as logic, integrity, courage, jealousy, resentment and discrimination. All of these different aspects and many more have combined to make us the version of ourselves that walks the earth today, and the same can be said for everyone else. We are a unique product of what we have been through and we operate from that place at all times. As we grow and evolve, gather more experiences and such, we adapt to who we are and then come from that place. Some people don't evolve because their psychology is fixed and their experiences are very limited. These people will come from a far narrower understanding of the world or bigger picture, but are still doing the very best they can with what they have available to them.

It's from this unique place of 'who we are' that we make decisions and take action. It's also the place that filters incoming information as we process it and integrates it into our reality on an ongoing basis. If someone is coming from a narrowed and closed perspective, which perhaps includes some sabotaging beliefs, that means new information is not received openly. This will be very different to someone who has grown to see the value of a different perspective.

I sometimes wonder if you can expect an unconscious person to make a conscious decision or have a conscious standpoint. The conclusion I have come to is that we can only work with what we've got and it would be like asking someone colour blind to see in colour. They simply are not wired up to do it, and so the request becomes unfair. In moments like this, be the mirror. Be the reflection of what consciousness, love, forgiveness and compassion can do. We are all therefore doing the best we can, and your version of "best" will differ from others. The reactions, opinions and behaviour of others will not always align with ours. And judging them for this is us being unconscious. Having compassion is seeing that they are doing their best, even when we are hurt or disappointed. Be the reflection of what consciousness, love, forgiveness and compassion can do.

Forgiveness sometimes needs something physical to mark its occurrence, or at least the intention that it is occurring (and believe me, when I say that even getting to the edge of forgiveness and at least wanting to do it can be massive progress). Only you know what feels right to you when the time comes. Once you have done your own work in knowing that the person involved was in fact doing their best, and you've looked back over the situation to check that you haven't made it mean something that it didn't, then it's time to forgive.

Look for an act or representation of forgiveness that will help you the most, but cost you the least. When I say cost I mean think it through consciously. If you feel like you want to call someone up and give them a piece of your mind, what would that cost you?

Time, energy, emotional pain, family fallout, drama, you being labelled as the troublemaker, further damage to other relationships that will be affected? Once you know what it's going to cost, it's up to you to work out if that cost is too high.

Is there another way you can feel relief and mark this moment of forgiveness that has a lesser cost attached to it? Is it enough, for example, that you write a letter to this person and burn it, bury it or tear it up and flush it down a toilet? Do you need to spend some time in meditation and ask to meet a version of this person's higher self in order to get the apology that you are not going to get on earth? Perhaps you need to put flowers on a grave, or donate to a charity. An act of kindness may represent a squaring up for you, or the chance to finally speak your mind and tell your story.

Whatever you choose, make sure it helps you the most but costs you the least. As soon as you can, find out what or who you need to forgive and get started. Because you can't change what happened but you can stop it from having a hold on you now.

And you are worthy of releasing this, you really are.

Who and what do you need to forgive in your life?

Which feelings and experiences might you be hanging on in order to fuel your inner victim and ego?

What do you need to do in order to free yourself?

"I AM walking free from my history. I forgive myself and others and release past hurt and trauma now. I love myself enough to free myself."

"Healing your wounds, living consciously and showing up in your own life are three of the most powerful things you can do to help yourself and everyone else."

~ Kate Spencer

LESSON 9

You can't fix other people

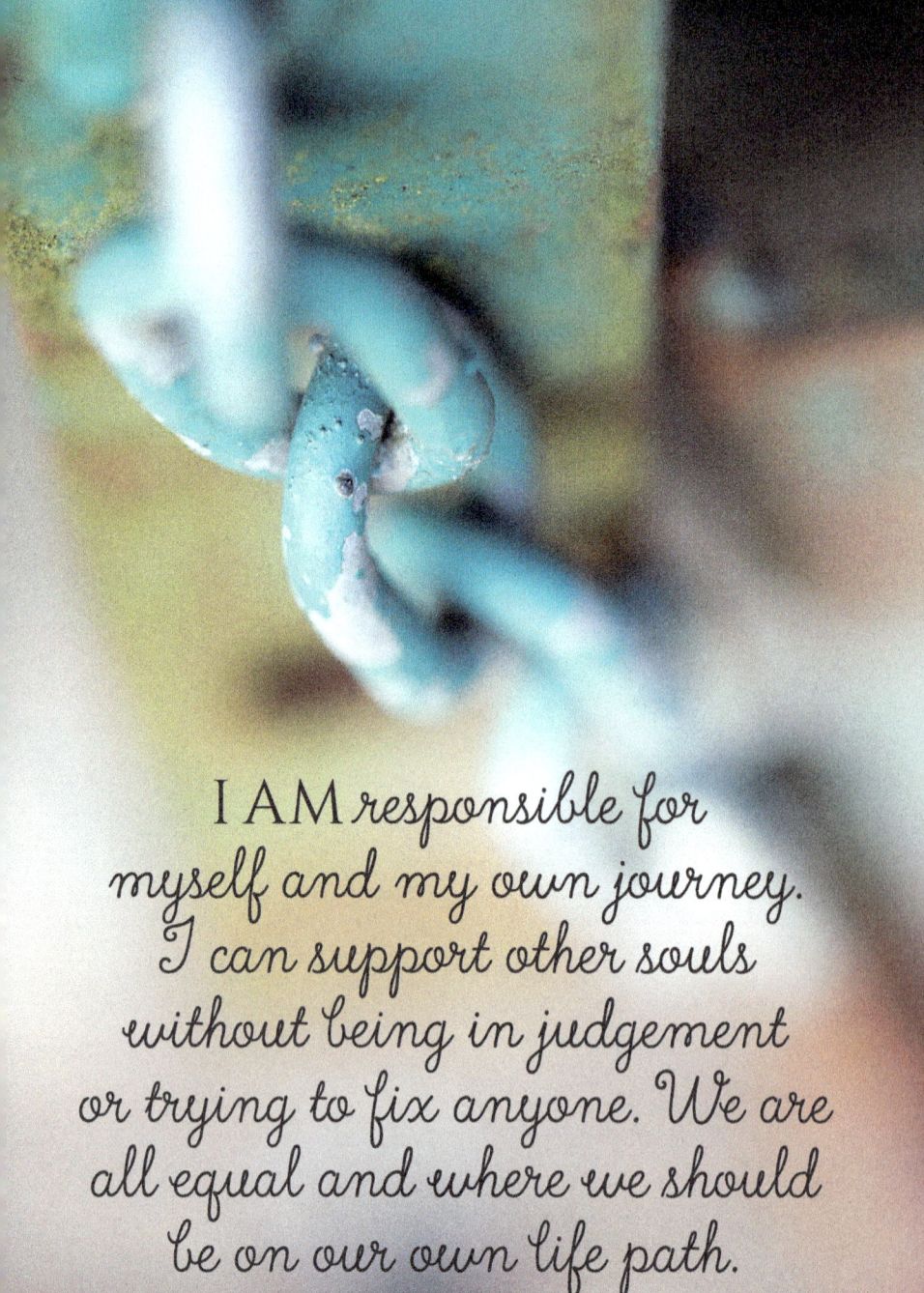

I AM responsible for myself and my own journey. I can support other souls without being in judgement or trying to fix anyone. We are all equal and where we should be on our own life path.

Lesson 9
Acceptance ~ You Can't Fix Other People

~ You are your own best chance, and that goes for all of us ~ Kate Spencer

When you are a big-hearted soul and start to live more consciously, it's a normal side effect to want to help other people. You start to see life from a different perspective, as you process your lessons and heal your wounds. More joy, peace and happiness come in as you learn about yourself and life, and what once may have felt like a black and white world is now in glorious technicolour.

My awakening was rapid, and I wanted badly to help other people to see what they had been missing. Although very well intended, my idea of helping people was initially not exactly that. I had slipped into fixing mode. The epiphanies that I'd had were giving me a different perspective on life, one that was helping me to make progress and evolve. My insights, lessons, experiences and evolution were happening in accordance with what I needed, and the life that I was creating. They were not a one size fits all solution for everyone, and by trying to overlay my stuff on someone else's life I was becoming a fixer.

People don't like being fixed, including you. Uninvited opinion and telling others what they should do isn't a good idea, unless they are at risk of harming themselves or other people, and here's why. People awaken when they are ready (and some never will) and we all have to take responsibility for our own lives. We all came here with a path to walk and lessons to learn, and by telling people what they should do not only are you being controlling (and this comes from fear), you are also stopping them from experiencing what they need to. Fixing someone all of the time sends out a vibrational subtext that they are not allowed to run their own life, and that, actually, you know what's best for them. Although you are not meaning to do it, this is very much coming from ego and can sabotage another soul's progress as well as undermine their confidence in a subtle yet real way when it comes to making their own decisions.

What if the lesson that they have coming up is going to be the making of them? And what if you stopping them from going through this or being a fixer throws them off course and they miss it? What if the lesson has simply been delayed and it's going to come around later and be harder in the future? I'm not saying here that you can't help people and guide them, but there is a big difference here between that and fixing.

Fixing someone comes from ego and a subtext of you knowing better than them. It's an energy of superiority and control, and you'll know that you have slipped into it because you will start to attract examples of people trying to fix you. Like with a lot of things, being conscious is the key here. Ask yourself what your motive is in helping someone, and then ask yourself what your real motive is. Get underneath the behaviour that you justify with the standard response that you "Want to help them" and see if you are, in fact, getting a payoff. Payoffs include being right, being in control, feeling superior and so on. These won't come up straightaway because they are not traits that we like to admit to, but if you want to evolve and stop fixing, then be honest with yourself.

Step back and breathe. Know that you can be supportive to another soul in different ways, that doesn't include fixing and are more empowering for both of you. Cheer them on from the side lines but allow them to manage their own life in their own way. Be a messenger and direct to information that may help, but know that it's up to them to take it or leave it and attach no meaning to this outcome. Be a mirror and reflection of what you have done, applied or executed in your own life and let them see how it's improved things for you. Shine your light and your truth in a non-egotistical way as an example of what can be, with the love and intention that they take what they need, and you have faith in this.

Appreciate that some people may have come to earth to help us all to learn. Perhaps they have soul contracts in place to act as a reflection in this lifetime to others, and show them traits that will illuminate where we need to do our work. Maybe by being "fixed" they would ruin the mirror they hold up for many and the ripple of change they are here to spread. Hold everyone in the energy of intention that they are doing the best they can and evolving for their highest good. This honours your journey as well as theirs.

This is especially important if you are working as a healer or a therapist. Holding the intention that you are there to help and support people to help themselves is paramount. It's also unethical and untrue for anyone to claim that they can heal or fix anyone else, as therapists and healers we hold space and act as a conduit for the work to occur. We might have skills that facilitate this process, but let's not live in our ego and set ourselves up as being the next Messiah.

If you come from a place fixing people, then you will attract people who are unwilling to take responsibility for their own healing and progress. This could end up in a whole lot of different scenarios. They may blame you for not helping them, or they may keep returning time after time for the same or similar issues and leave you frustrated and drained.

Make sure you let people know that you are a catalyst for their own change, a support to their own healing and transformation. This will empower you both and often means that the healing is more profound and happens quicker. If you meet someone that wants or expects you to fix them it's really important to be clear and honest about the fact that you can't. However you may well be able to support them and hold space for them, and offer effective therapy to empower them to fix themselves.

A note on the Ask Hole. There are people that exist who are very entrenched in their own story and enjoy the attention they receive for being stuck in their stuff. They may not be aware that they are stuck, but you'll be aware – mainly because you get the same account of how awful life is every time you engage with them. In order to keep you hooked into the scenario of giving them attention and endorsing their poor me archetype, they will seek your "advice". A part of you will be relieved because if they have asked, you're not fixing! Perhaps you can shed some light on their situation that will truly help them again. The trouble is that they never listen or action anything. This is because the payoff of getting your sympathy and undivided attention is way bigger for them than actually making the changes that they say they want in their life.

My advice is this, be present and have compassion, listen carefully and when asked for advice, give it once and give it clearly. After that moment, again with compassion, refer back to your previous exchange and say with a whole lot of love "You know what I think". Hopefully once the payoff stops they will be more inclined to make positive change that will serve them.

Who have you been trying to fix?

Why do you feel the need to fix them?

How are you going to work on yourself to stop being a fixer?

"I AM responsible for myself and my own journey. I can support other souls without being in judgement or trying to fix anyone. We are all equal and where we should be on our own life path."

LESSON 10

Intuition and signs

I AM open to the signs and signals that the universe is sending me, I take positive action in the light of these.

Lesson 10
Signs & Serendipity

~ Synchronicities are pebbles dropped by the Universe to signpost you on your journey through life ~ Dot Elliot

Once you start to align your energy and consciousness with what you want to create, the Universe will start to respond to your request and send you signs and signals that will guide you. These are clues as to what action you should take (or in some cases not take) and will come into your life as a response to your intentions. This is where it is important to have strong over-arching intentions that are general enough to help you in your life overall, as well as the specific intentions of what you are wanting to manifest and draw in. By this I mean fostering beliefs for yourself that are aligned to everything unfolding perfectly for you, all being well and the Universe supporting your journey here as a soul.

As you send these intentions and feelings out, you'll be drawing in matching experiences along the way, as well as occurrences that may appear to be co-incidental, but when you tune into them and take any inspired action your gut tells you to, could lead you in the perfect direction. This can feel a bit like painting by numbers. You know what that section should look like right now, but you can't see the whole. The Universe might throw you some additional scenes that you hadn't considered at the outset, and when these come up you may feel that they are spoiling the vision that you are holding dear. Don't get disheartened – refer back to your general belief that all is working out in accordance with your highest good. Trust your gut feeling along the way, but know that all is well.

What we see as 'random' occurrences and interactions are actually nothing of the kind, they are the Universe signposting you towards what you need to do and experience in order to get what you have asked for. Behind the scenes of your human awareness the dots are joining up. Have faith that the Universe has heard your request and started to line up matching frequencies to help you to draw in your vision. Between the person you are now and the person you need to be in order to live in this new reality that you are asking for, there may be some things you need to learn, some people you need to connect with or a trait you need to develop.

The Universe will naturally start to plug any gaps that you need to fill behind the scenes, like your own personal cosmic assistant. You may not realise in your conscious mind that you need these parts of the puzzle, but as part of you asking vibrationally for the outcome you want, there may be things that have to occur as part of the lining up. Signs and serendipity could lead you to the people and situations you need to help you progress.

So how will you know if it's a sign? There are two things to look for: your gut feeling and repetition. If you get a strong gut feeling or a pull towards something that is seemingly random, the likelihood is that it's a sign. Intuition is resonance, it's the pull towards a person, place or thing because there is energetic attraction at that time, it is also something that we can't justify logically and this sometimes makes us ignore it. When you look back over your life you may be able to pinpoint moments when you didn't follow your intuition and you wish you had. It's an innate superpower and the more you practise it the stronger it gets.

Simple things like asking your intuition who is calling when you hear the phone ring will help you to practise and be more open. Repetition is the same sign coming into your awareness, until you get the message. It could be the same thing in a different form such as an article in a magazine about yoga, a yoga teacher being interviewed on television as you skip channels and a flyer coming through your door about a class starting locally. I always think that three especially is a magic number and when something crosses my path three times it's definitely time to take notice.

What does the sign mean? Firstly I will say that it means whatever they mean to you. This isn't a cop out, it's the truth. The Universe, your own intuition, your guides and more will communicate with you in a way that gets your attention and is meant to pass on information to you. There are, of course, some generic interpretations, such as a white feather usually being associated with having Angels close by. Of course take these on board, but in the main I would encourage you to see what something means to you, in your frame of reference and in your heart.

I would look at dream interpretation in the same way, and sometimes a dream can be a sign too. There may be standard concepts and associations you can consider when thinking about a dream that you feel may contain a message for you, but putting down your dream book and tuning into yourself to find your own interpretation can be more insightful. Once you have tuned into the signs that you are getting and what they mean, it's time to take any inspired action that you feel drawn to.

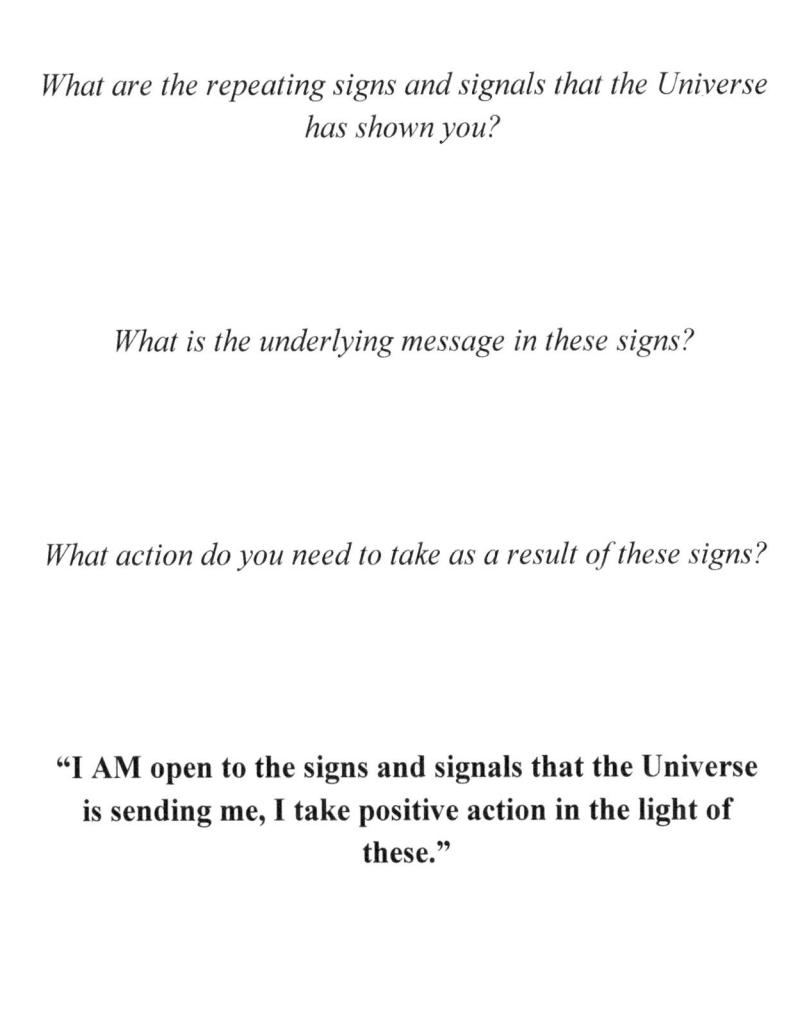

What are the repeating signs and signals that the Universe has shown you?

What is the underlying message in these signs?

What action do you need to take as a result of these signs?

"I AM open to the signs and signals that the Universe is sending me, I take positive action in the light of these."

"Be who you are and say what you feel,
because those who mind don't matter,
and those who matter don't mind."

~ Dr Seuss

LESSON 11

Self love and loving others

I AM lovable, I love myself and my life experience reflects this back to me in every moment.

Lesson 11
Love Yourself

~ To love oneself is the beginning of a lifelong romance ~ Oscar Wilde

The more I observe, the more I think we've got the wrong idea about self-love. We are caught in a space and time where we are moving from an old paradigm into a new one, and we are struggling to find a balance that works. In the not too distant past, the woman of the house was expected to be the caregiver. They looked after their husband, home and children and it was considered both a noble and kind role to occupy. Always putting others first, and by default putting yourself last. This was being "selfless" and was not only expected, but encouraged by society. Times changed and so did gender roles. Childcare, creating income and looking after the home are now shared, in the main, or if not shared this is more of a choice for the people involved than a given like in the past.

We've broken free from that old paradigm where women stayed at home and put everyone's needs ahead of theirs, and rightfully so. But a cultural hangover remains. When a woman is seen to care for herself and love herself, some of us view this as selfish still. I've heard whisperings on the playground of "who does she think she is" when another mum announces that she's going on holiday with the girls. Yet the same people who whisper would never pull a man down for going away for a long weekend golfing. A woman exercising self-love can be observed by others as being egotistical and selfish, but it is usually perceived this way by those who are still stuck in an old way of thinking. They have not yet found a way to break out of this and get peaceful about loving themselves yet, and since this is not a part of their reality and experience, they perhaps don't see the value in it yet.

We need to find the balance between the old concepts of putting ourselves last and the skewed perception that loving and looking after yourself is selfish. Learning to love yourself is hugely important. I'm not talking here about the fake "loving yourself" that broken people project out into the world in order to show up and feel good enough. I'm talking about a deep acceptance that you are a work in progress who has plenty of human moments and failings but you know that you are a good human worthy of love. A work in progress who is doing their best with what they've got.

Self-love is the cornerstone of your life. It's going to massively improve your experiences and relationships. It's not arrogant or selfish to love who you are, it's necessary. Without this you cannot hope to manifest the life you dream of. The vibrational subtext to self-love is "I AM worthy of all things good", and when you don't love yourself or feel worthy you'll be sending out an energy aligned to "I AM not worthy of anything good". You can see how each belief will attract in matching energy, and I know which one serves you best and will create resistance to positive energy and act as a magnet to the negative.

The journey to self-love is can be challenging. To love yourself means accepting who you are, forgiving yourself, speaking to yourself in kind and encouraging ways, looking after your body, having healthy boundaries. It's about being at peace with you in all ways, including past, present and future versions. The more self-love you can generate, the more you can let go of other people's opinions of you and see them as their stuff, not yours.

Our personal and intimate relationships are great testimonies to how we feel about ourselves. When we are prepared to step out of them and observe the patterns that we have attracted, they can be very illuminating about where we are at as individuals. Look at the experiences that you have drawn to you, and they will show you where you are resonating in terms of your own self-love.

I know from my past that living in an energy of 'not feeling good enough' will be matched up to people and situations that give you a whole lot more of not feeling good enough. When I was in a place of not loving myself I drew in people that didn't love me either, and the more I blamed myself for things going bad, the more I attracted criticism from others and believed that I was the cause. For me, this was a situation that lasted far too long, and so chronically low was my own self-love that I actually had to be pushed out of it kicking and screaming. I started to work on loving me and my life started to change in positive ways. I began to see the correlation between how I thought and felt about myself, and my experience. You attract what you are, and I couldn't draw love in until I started to feel it. Thankfully this happened for me, and it can happen for you too.

Self-love can also help you with all aspects of your life because the underlying vibration is "I AM worthy of being treated with love". This starts to line things up in accordance with this frequency, and you will begin to experience more love in your life which will also mean more happiness, joy and wellbeing. When you love yourself you treat yourself better, you naturally want the best for yourself. This can mean improvements in the way that you eat, your friendships, better boundaries, more self-care and other behavioural acts that protect your energy and self-esteem. All of these things are a side effect of self-love and all will raise your vibration, make you feel better and help you to attract more of what you want in your life.

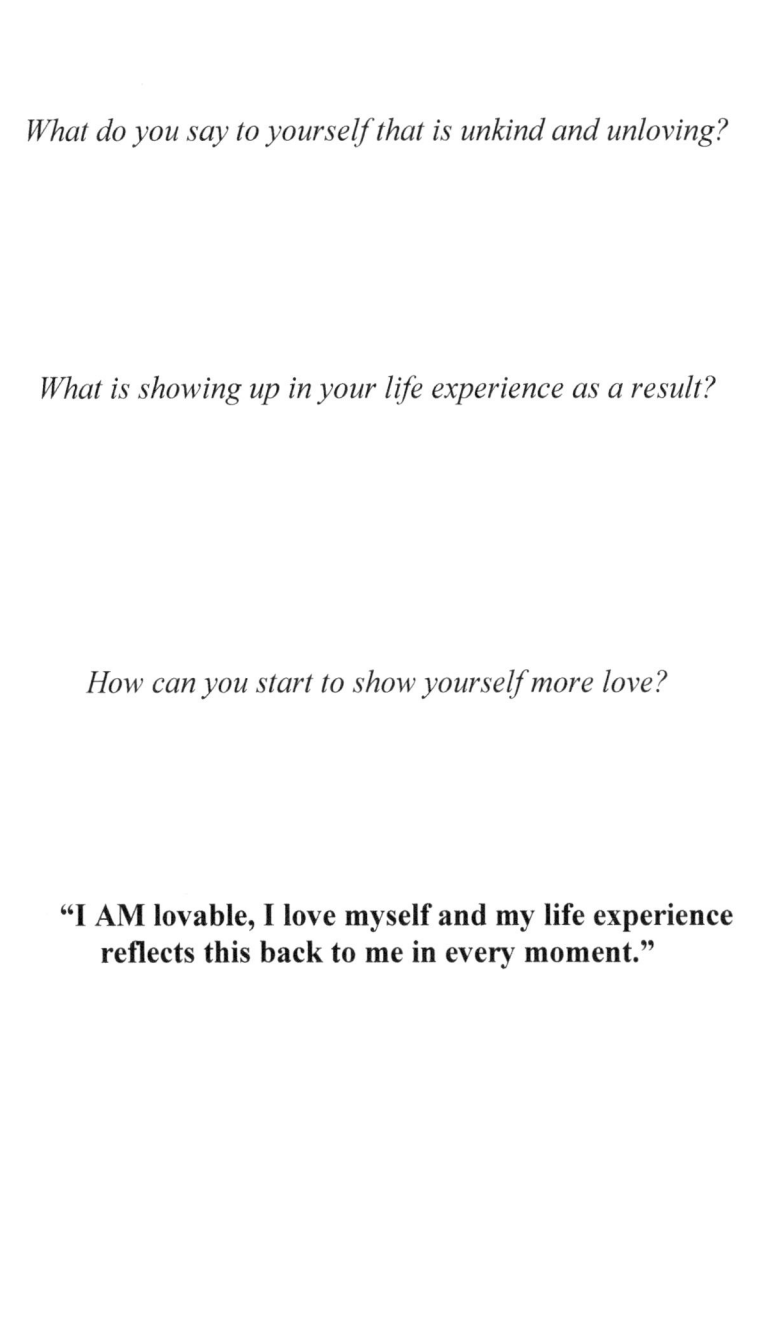

What do you say to yourself that is unkind and unloving?

What is showing up in your life experience as a result?

How can you start to show yourself more love?

"I AM lovable, I love myself and my life experience reflects this back to me in every moment."

"I believe that tomorrow is another day,
and I believe in miracles."

~ Audrey Hepburn

LESSON 12

Allow the flow

I AM living in the flow of life and all good things and experiences flow to me easily. I AM releasing any and all resistance to my flow.

Lesson 12
The Flow ~ Release Resistance and Allow the Flow of Goodness

~It took getting truly lost, for me to truly start to find my way ~ Claire McLaren

There is a Flow of energy that exists in life where all things are available to us in any moment. We can align with it and create the life and experiences we desire. The phrase "Go with The Flow" reminds us of how it feels when things seem to happen with grace and ease.

Being in The Flow means being connected to All That Is. Living in joy and abundance and having what we need in the moment. There is an acceptance that all is well and life is good, with more goodness coming. People in the flow surrender to life and know that life is occurring as it should be, all that comes their way is in perfect time and for their greatest and highest good. A quiet and steadfast faith that all is well, and when you are sending this out as your dominant vibration, it certainly is. If only it were that easy though!

I have experienced pockets of Flow, and I strive for these moments in time to get longer and more frequent. I say this so that you know you are not a failure if you are the same. Our human lives make it hard to live in this energy all or most of the time. I love the feeling and I ideally want to live there, but it's sometimes hard to surrender. When you are in that Flow, life is easier, and this makes it ironic when it's not easy to get into in the first place. Frustration will bring in more resistance, and then we end up keeping it at bay even more. It's an energy that you have to ease into, not one that you can summon up and control.

We are more familiar with the feeling of not being in Flow. Those days when things don't go our way, and we feel out of synch, good fortune and opportunity disappear. Obstacles, challenges manifest in our life, relationships and body. Lack of Flow makes you feel stuck and the more stuck you feel, the more stuck you are. We know this is because we are feeling the energy and associated emotions of being stuck and this keeps us in a kind of holding pattern, attracting more.

One of the things you can do if you find this going on with yourself is to consciously step back and work on changing how you feel. Being aware that you are stuck or out of Flow is the first thing you need to do, and then after that don't get mad at yourself, surrender. Know that this is your starting point of getting back into Flow and if you end up beating yourself up about it you are going to create more low vibration emotions that will, in turn, create more resistance.

Simple and quick ways to raise your vibration away from resistance include getting into deliberate gratitude, perhaps a guided meditation would help or a conscious shift of your thoughts towards what you can give thanks for. Music and laughter can also be very helpful, it's good to find a clip or two that's going to make you chuckle or a piece of music that reminds you of something good. These are quick fixes to help you to get unstuck long enough to start doing some work on releasing your resistance, and although it can feel like a monumental task, sometimes it's actually just a thought or intention away once you start to get some traction.

We know that Lack of Flow is created by resistance. We don't do it deliberately, but it happens when we block the good stuff coming our way. The emotions that manifest resistance are low in vibration and include jealousy, anger, resentment and fear. They create metaphorical rocks in the river of Flow, stopping the good energy reaching us even though it is available in abundance. Think for a moment about your own life and an area where things could be better. This could be relationships, health, finances and beyond. Now take a conscious step back from the situation and look at it from a perspective of where you could be creating resistance.

Where are you in fear? What are you saying to yourself about this situation? What are the negative emotions and feelings that come up around this? We create stories and beliefs that may not be true, and we stick to them creating self-sabotage. Can you see where you are creating resistance in this situation and how your thoughts, feelings and consciousness have created blockages in your Flow? Perhaps there is so much fear and resistance that a dam has been built across your Flow, and stopped goodness coming in for you altogether? Becoming conscious about where you are creating resistance without self-judgment can help you to release resistance and get back into Flow. Generally keeping your vibration as high as possible also helps you to flow better, so look to engage in good self-care, cut etheric cords regularly and stay out of drama and low vibe emotions as best you can. Another important principle of The Flow is Fair Exchange. This is about the giving and receiving of energy in equal proportion wherever you can, because when you are out of exchange you are out of Flow.

This goes for all kinds of energy, not just paying for goods and services. When someone does something kind for you, pass the kindness on when you can. If someone is supportive of you, either give them that back in exchange when they need it or pay it back by offering support to a person or cause somewhere down the line. Giving and receiving of energy in equal measure is a good overall intention to help you stay in The Flow. This can get confusing when things are free.

There is a good giving energy behind a charitable donation or a genuine intention to want to help someone, and often when I do repayment I'll ask that they pay the good deed forward at some point in time when they are able. This keeps everyone in fair exchange, and the value of what I gave and what they give does not have to be the same, it just has to help someone. This is different to being out of exchange with someone when they say that something is "free" but there is actually an underlying energetic cost and obligation created. I am bringing this up here because it's something that I have noticed happening in spiritual circles, and in my opinion it's not conducive to Flow and positive energy.

When someone appears to give freely all of the time and accept nothing in return, they can be coming from lack. Their "generosity" shows you that they have no regard for their own time or energy and therefore choose not to value themselves. Remember also that Flow is giving and receiving. It is my opinion that an energy exchange should be honoured wherever possible to keep both parties in Flow with the Universe. When someone continually stops you from making an exchange, they are keeping you out of Flow. I know that there are people out there who do some good giving back, and I am cheering them on. That's not what I am talking about here.

I'm saying always strive to be in Fair Exchange and ask if there is an ulterior motive. The energy on earth is changing and many "leaders" who have positioned themselves as such are being show to be people who are not ready for the task. They are too entrenched in ego and their old wounds are not healed. If you tune in you'll feel this and start to see behind the mask. I don't say this to elevate myself and would refer you back to the beginning of this book where I talk about taking what you need and knowing what is right for you.

Let's expand that into knowing who is right for you too. Giving you something for "Free" puts you in an energy of obligation. The more "Free" time, energy or access you get, the more you feel like you owe this person.

This makes you vulnerable in lots of ways including being sold to and being emotionally manipulated. I don't know of any genuine conscious or spiritual person that would do this. For one, they would not want to be out of exchange themselves and secondly they would not want to set up an energy deficit that controlled others.

I know of people who have been so desperate for ego glory that they have literally run themselves into the ground and become ill offering their "Free" services to others. This "Free" service ultimately became a way of herding people together to manipulate them and sell to them, by which time people felt like they were in so much energetic debt that they were afraid to leave. This is both unethical and it's working against the Universal Laws. Exercise discernment, things are shifting and the veils are dropping now as the vibration on earth changes and we move into another way of being.

More people are coming through that say they can help you but are actually wanting or needing something else. The compassionate part of me would like to think they are not conscious of this, but that doesn't make it any less harmful to those who get caught up. Always look behind the behaviour and ask yourself what is driving it before you get involved and carried away. Protect your energy, make good choices and look to stay in Fair Exchange.

Where is my life not flowing right now?

What is the fear that is creating the resistance in my flow?

What can I do to release this fear and allow more goodness to flow to me?

"I AM living in the flow of life and all good things and experiences flow to me easily. I AM releasing any and all resistance to my flow."

"Be happy with what you have, while working for what you want."

~ Helen Keller

LESSON 13

Life and soul lessons

I AM grateful for all of my lessons and the gifts that they bring me for my growth and evolution as a soul on earth.

Lesson 13
Lessons ~ Life and Soul Lessons

~ Some people come in our life as blessings, some people come in as lessons ~Mother Teresa

Life is full of lessons, and they begin as soon as we get here. Some are general life lessons that we have to get our head around pretty quickly in order to survive, socialise and function in society, and others are specific to us. Our parents are our first teachers in the school of life, and show us how the world works according to them.

One of the lessons that we learn later as adults is that our parents teach us from their perspective and belief system, and sometimes this doesn't serve who we are. This may be because in a fast-changing world, some of what they teach us is no longer relevant by the time we reach adulthood. The other reason is that they are sharing lessons from their own consciousness, some of which may be limiting to them as individuals and to us if we integrate them into our own psychology. Even if the things that our parents teach us are not helpful as we grow, they were gifted to us with love and good intention at the time.

In addition to general lessons, I believe that we all come to earth with a unique soul curriculum full of lessons that are specific to us. When you begin to live a life more conscious, you are sending out an intention to the Universe that you want to heal and evolve. The Universe hears this as your overall intention and starts to help you out by sending you the lessons that you need to achieve this. Think about it in terms of Law of Attraction – your ultimate outcome is to be more enlightened, and in order to get there, the Universe needs to start joining up some dots. You need to experience some more earthly lessons in order to evolve, and by walking a more spiritual path in life, you can find that lessons are accelerated to help you progress faster.

What does it mean when the lesson comes back? Repeating lessons usually happens because we are not learning what we need to. Perhaps we don't understand the essence of the lesson that's playing out, so life brings them around again. This is why so many of us seem to attract a different version of the same situation time and time again – we have not learned what we were supposed to in order to help us. This can be frustrating, but getting frustrated will only create resistance and block your learning even more.

Try to stand back, get centred and look at the situation from a higher-self perspective. Ask yourself what you are missing here. What do you need to learn or to heal? Meditate on this, and trust in your intuition. Look for the signs and signals that the Universe is sending you to help you understand and navigate your way through the lesson. It is also important to know that just as we have our own soul curriculum, as do others.

This means they are experiencing situations in their lives that are great learning opportunities, specific to them. The kind-hearted person that you are may want to charge in and rescue them when a lesson unleashes its heartache and struggle, especially if it is someone you love. I'm not going to say don't help, but I am going to say that it is important not to rescue. Allow them the learning they need from the situation, and if a full-on rescue is unavoidable, then perhaps their lesson is wrapped up in gratitude, humility, faith in humanity or taking responsibility.

Always know that each one of us is here to experience, learn and grow as a soul, and never rob someone of that opportunity, no matter how well-meaning you are. Hold an intention that you are empowering both of you. Be kind but also be respectful of their learning as well as your own. Lessons are the gift that won't feel like a gift in the moment. They can be wrapped up in struggle and pain, and can make you feel like you are drowning in a sea of overwhelm and desperation. They can whip up such a storm in your life that you feel wholly battle-scarred and mangled beyond belief.

Life Lessons change us on many levels, but the change really comes from the processing, the healing and the personal journey that each experience offers you. We have the choice to come out of the storm a different person, and although our exterior may be as fragile as spun sugar, the fire we have walked through has forged a strength deep inside of us that is evident in time.

In my experience the greater the lesson is, the bigger the gift is too. Keep this as your focus when you face something really challenging, and know that even when you can't see it, the gift will appear in time. Start seeing your challenges on earth as lessons, and find it in your heart to be grateful for them, or at least hold the intention that one day you will be able to. Notice when lessons come up, and work hard to stay out of the Drama that so many of them can create. Step back, and ask for the essence of the lesson, why it is playing out and what it is teaching you. Go deep within yourself and be honest about your human moments and what you can improve on, how is life supporting and guiding you towards a better version of yourself?

Lessons are often multi-faceted, because you are usually sharing them with another person or people in your life. The same lesson can be a completely unique experience for the people involved, as they work through it from their own perspective. When sharing a lesson, honour both or all of you as best you can. Know that this or these souls have stepped forwards to help you at this time, and you have to help them, even if it feels that this is not the case. Detach from the human aspects of what is playing out and look for the essence of the lesson from your Higher Self.

Act with love and compassion as best you can, forgive your human moments and know that the gift will reveal itself in due course.

What life lessons have I experienced so far?

What was the gift in these lessons?

How will these lessons help me to move forward?

"I AM grateful for all of my lessons and the gifts that they bring me for my growth and evolution as a soul on earth."

"May every sunrise hold more promise,
and every sunset hold more peace."

~ Unknown

LESSON 14

Be here now

I AM present, fully connected to myself and the earth and enjoying every moment as it unfolds in the here and now.

Lesson 14
Being Present

~ The thing that we forget is that our time is precisely that. It's ours. And we get to choose how we want to use it ~ Sarah Cornforth

Being able to be fully present is a gift to the people around you and will serve you in so many ways in your life. We know this intellectually and intuitively, and we can feel it when we are in the company of someone who isn't present with us. Maybe we can't name it initially, but we pick up the vibe that they are distracted. Everything that you give your energy to that is not in the present moment is going to rob you of the quality of that moment. And life is made up of moments, your past is a collection of moments and so is your future, and they all started in the moment that we call now.

Modern technology can hugely sabotage being present. We live in a world where we are more connected than ever through mobile phones, the internet and social media – yet this ironically often disconnects us from the people that are sitting right in front of us. The fear of missing out (and there is even an acronym for that because it's such an epidemic – FOMO) drives a constant need to be "checking my phone". Checking it for what exactly? What your friend has made for dinner, who's booked a holiday or funny cat clips? Or perhaps you'll see harrowing stories about the state of the world that you cannot change and will pull on your heart and your energy hugely and knock your vibration for the rest of the day? Political fears, opinions and judgments, fake news, clickbait, the list goes on. If this is you then be conscious of it, and do what you can to change the virtual habit that is stopping you from connecting for real.

I am not naïve enough to think that it's possible to be fully present all of the time. Life happens and distractions come along that we cannot avoid, but don't make this a spiritual excuse. So what if you can't achieve it all of the time? You can make a massive difference in your life and in the life of others if you simply get better at it, and I know you can. Being conscious of where you are in a given moment is the start. We often allow our awareness to be pulled into the past or pushed forwards into the future. The past has gone, and the only power that it has over us is the way that we feel about it in the now time. The future is, as yet, unwritten and the only power we have to do that is in the now time – so where is the most productive place to be? The present moment, and it is the place where you can influence everything.

The past is often the territory of unresolved wounds and trauma, missed opportunities and failed relationships. When we look back, we forget that we are a work in progress like everyone else on the planet. We judge who we used to be from our current, more evolved standpoint and frame of reference and we forget that the whole point of life is to learn and experience (and that we're never done.) When you look at life this way it's obvious that the longer you're in the game, the more you're going to learn and the more experience you are going to bank. The decisions that you made in the past may trigger feelings such as regret or embarrassment now, but at the time they were the best that you could do. The past is just that – past. We can't change what happened there, but we can change the way we perceive it and how much time we spend there. It is not helpful to trigger feelings in the now, that are brought about by something you can't change. Remember that Law of Attraction responds to how you feel. When you dwell on something that makes you feel bad in any way, your vibration is lowered and you send that vibe out to the Universe.

A note on reminiscing – this can bring you a greater connection in the present moment with the people that you shared your history with. Looking back over occasions and moments can be touching and create a deep sense of love and belonging, sometimes across generations. This can bring the energy of love and gratitude into the present moment as well as strengthening identity, purpose and foundations for us, especially children. But it's the way that the past makes you feel that is relevant here. The emotions that you associate with it will be the vibration that it creates in you in the now, and how it affects you emotionally and energetically.

If you know that your attention is being pulled back to something in your past that feels painful, uncomfortable or unresolved, then there is some healing to do here. You may be able to find a safe space and do this on your own (perhaps Lesson 2 and shadow work would help), or you may need some appropriate support. Know that whatever this wound is, you are allowing it to rob you of experiencing joy in the present moment if you don't take some kind of action to heal it, and you are so worthy of having a life that you love instead of one with a subtext of feeling unworthy in some way. Find out what needs to be healed, and do something to start the process.

Spending time in your mind on a perpetual loop of fast forward can be equally unhelpful, and in an age of vision boards and Law of Attraction has become something of a modern-day curse. The future may be the land of possibility, and place of hopes and dreams and goals not yet realised, but it is also the place of "if only". This feeling that stops us being satisfied with what we have right now and triggers a feeling of lack, which the Universe picks up vibrationally as resistance and blocks our flow.

Wanting stuff in the future can stop it from coming into your experience, because you are sending out a vibrational subtext of "things will be ok when", and we all fill in the blanks with what it is we want to experience. When we get a promotion, when we meet the love of our life, when we finally lose weight, when we graduate, when we can leave our job, and so on. Living in the future is always holding what we want at arm's length, and it always will.

This doesn't mean that you shouldn't have goals, plans and a bucket list. But it does mean that getting conscious about what you are sending out there is important, and you can only know that in the present moment. Remember I said earlier that you must make things vibrationally accessible to you if you want to create them? In other words you have to send out a matching frequency by feeling that this experience is happening now. If you can't access that feeling you can't draw it in, and worse still you may slip into a feeling like "as if that's ever going to happen for me" and unintentionally create resistance. Being present with yourself - we live our lives at a far faster pace than our ancestors, and the constant stream of information we receive contributes to us feeling overwhelmed, overstimulated and overloaded. There is always something that needs to be done, and in the middle of our whirlwind we forget of existence, to get into the eye of the storm and be present with ourselves.

As Within, So Without. Everything in your life started with you, and everything that is coming starts with you too. We need time and space to breathe, to step off the treadmill of life and be with ourselves. If you don't get your head and heart around who you are and what you want in your life, what you need to heal and how you want to live – then you're going to be swept along with the masses and life is going to happen to you. Time is going to pass anyway, and you are going to get older regardless. And one day you might look back and wonder where all of the time went, and how the heck did it all end up like this? And we already know that feeling, the car journey that we take when we are not present and we drive on auto pilot, when we get to the destination we can't remember getting there. Don't allow this to happen to your life, because for most of us it is.

Time is like money, but more precious. You can only ever spend it once. Unlike money, though, you don't get a heads up that it's going to run out. Find time to be present with yourself, and work on making it a habit. Checking in with what is happening in your life, your body, your emotions and reviewing what's working and what's not. This will allow you to become aware of changes that need to be made in order to help yourself and those around you. Combine this with an overall intention of being more present in your life generally and fostering a conscious awareness of moments when you aren't. Learn some gentle and loving techniques to bring you back to the now, and practice them when you need to. As you do, this will become easier and more automatic.

Creating a daily habit for being present can bring a whole new level of awareness to your life and the quality of it moment by moment. I like to take specific time in the morning whenever possible to be present with myself and set myself up for the day ahead. If this sounds like a huge task, it's not. It's minimal effort with maximum return, and the effect will compound and pay you dividends you may have never dreamed of. As with everything – do what works for you.

I like the habit of setting myself up for the day and then closing down my energy at night, it feels natural to me to have an ending and a beginning to each daily chapter of my life. I like to do what I can to choose my vibration at the start of the day and then reflect, give gratitude and call back my energy at night. I find that this helps to keep my energy clear as an ongoing practice and keeps me moving in the right direction. I get up early enough to do a ten-minute guided meditation and grounding every morning before my day starts. I follow that with a visualisation in the shower of releasing everything that does not serve me flowing down the plug hole.

I might even know what these things are, so I just intend this as a general outcome – but if I am working on releasing someone or something specific, down they go (with love and gratitude for the lessons, experiences and growth they brought me). I then ask, visualise or intend that the water is energised and as it flows over me I feel a sense of being protected and empowered, knowing that there is a strong energetic barrier around me to help me through the day to only attract what will serve me and in turn, the people I am here to serve. Once I am dressed I make a list of what I want to get done that day, and I prioritise the tasks. I include self-care prompts such as have enough water, eat as if you love yourself and do your best.

At night I practice good sleep hygiene whenever possible. I know that I need about eight hours of good quality sleep to function well and have enough energy for the things I need to get done. I don't watch or listen to the news, because I find it distressing and it fills me with pain and torment before I am trying to relax and close down my energy before bed. Some people may say that this avoidance is naïve, I would answer that by saying if I choose to look at any news I do it through the day and only when I am feeling emotionally resilient enough to not be affected personally. I am a huge giver and I help where I can, but I know myself well enough to know that this is not good for me to expose myself to energy that drains me, scares me and harms me when there is usually nothing I can do to change it. Me being floored with no energy and scared shitless is not going to help me or the people I came here to help, so no news for me before bed.

I choose crystals to put under my pillow, a drop of lavender on my pyjamas and I ask for all cords to be cut that do not serve me. I do a protection visualisation with some soft music playing in the background. I use the same piece every night so that I can create what is referred to as an "anchor", a type of psychological reference point that helps you to create a response within yourself. (You've probably experienced this before when you've heard a track playing on the radio that reminds you of a time in your life and you've felt a version of that feeling in the now.) I give gratitude for as much as I can, tell myself that I am doing a good job – especially when I feel like I haven't, and I snuggle up with the intention that I am having a healing and energising gorgeous full night's sleep. If you combine both the morning and night habits that I use they will take you about half an hour, and that includes the shower that you'll be having anyway.

When I have time (or when I choose to give myself more time) I may extend either or both habits and include journaling, reading something inspiring or exercise in the morning or stretches at night. I might also include some aspects of being present with myself during the day as well such as taking a mindful walk, with deep breaths and affirmations that align to the life that I am creating, a guided meditation, soft music and reflection or whatever feels right to do at that time.

The process of checking in with yourself and being present with you, gives you time and space to breathe, regroup and align. It's something that will change your vibration, your behaviour and your direction if you need to in any and all areas of your life. It's necessary to get off auto pilot and be more conscious if you want to make more of a positive difference. If you have resistance to being present with yourself this is likely to be rooted in fear of really looking at your life, or perhaps unworthiness where you are not able to give yourself the gift of time and space to improve and grow. If this is the case, it's going to be even more transformational if you can get behind these feelings and find a way to give this to yourself. The greater the resistance that you can overcome, the greater the gift you'll receive. Dig deep and find the courage to even just try your version of being present with yourself for one week, perhaps a morning and evening habit similar to mine that you can road test for real and see if it helps you, even just to prove me wrong.

Because I know that even in a short time you are going to feel a beneficial shift in your world, and it's likely you'll want to keep going.

.

What can I do to become more present?

Am I avoiding being present because I am struggling with something?

When do I tend to be least present and how can I change this?

"I AM present, fully connected to myself and the earth and enjoying every moment as it unfolds in the here and now."

LESSON 15

Discernment

I AM safe and free to exercise the power of choice over all parts of my life. I honour and respect myself by having discernment. I spend my precious time and energy with people and in situations that are in alignment with my greater good and who I AM.

Lesson 15
Empowered Choices ~ Discernment

~ Embrace your human being self along with your spiritual being experience. Because in essence they are the both the same ~
Nancy Melton-Morales

Discernment is the coming together of two things: awareness and choice. Awareness is about being conscious and learning what serves you, feels good and fits and conversely knowing what doesn't. Choice is what you do as a result of awareness. No one knows how you feel. You are unique, and so are your lessons and your journey. This means that you must learn to trust how things feel to you, and exercise discernment from a personal point of view. Just as you are working from your own unique perspective, so is everyone else.

You may meet someone that you don't feel comfortable around, and that is relevant to you. The same person might be best friends with someone you know and they think the world of them. Neither of you is wrong, you are both picking up energy in a unique way, and both of you can choose what you do with that information. There have been people that have dumped on me from a height, and I am sure you can say the same. They may not be bad people per se, but they are bad for me to be connected to. If someone asks me of my experience with them I will share appropriately and consciously, followed by the caveat that I believe it's important to speak as you find, and that they may find this person to be entirely different to me. The run-in or bad experience that I had with them may have been a lesson I had to learn, or it could have been something that I shared with their former self years ago when they were not as evolved as they were now, and the same can be said for me, of course. Just because this person is not for me does not mean that someone else will experience them this way. It does mean, however, that I need to exercise discernment if they come back onto my radar.

The gut feeling that we talk about is actually us picking up the vibration or frequency that someone is sending out, and when we feel uncomfortable it's usually because there is an energy mis-match with them and us. We are reading energy all of the time, some of us are more aware of this than others. When we feel an incongruence, things don't quite add up, make sense or seem entirely genuine but this feeling happens so quickly and is often intangible so it's really hard to verbalise and explain to others. Remember also that their experience of a person or place can be different to yours. We can't explain it or justify it, and this is when our human logical mind tries to talk us out of it.

The way you feel is valid, and you can usually rely on it as being so. Usually – because being in fear, low in emotional resilience, stressed or unwell can affect how accurate our awareness is. This makes way for another kind of discernment, where you need to be self-aware and know when you are having a potential off day. Avoid making decisions with a great deal of gravity based purely on how you feel if you are not in a clear energetic space and feeling good.

One recent example was when I was faced with deciding something on behalf of my child, and I was aware that I was being triggered by the subject matter and pushed into fear. I knew that by being fearful I would not be objective in decision making, and that I would only see what was in alignment with my current fear state. I couldn't get into the first part of discernment in a clear way, so my awareness would have been filtered, incomplete and fearful.

I asked someone in my life who I trust and know can look at this objectively to consider the situation, to weigh up the evidence and then come back to me with their balanced opinion and perspective. I received their insights openly, and then waited a few days until I had shored up my energy a bit more with good self-care. I reviewed the situation and included their opinion, bringing me a different conscious awareness. I then made my choice / decision from a place of empowerment not fear.

Discernment also means to have an awareness of which emotions and feelings belong to you, and what belongs to someone else. Sometimes what we think is someone else's vibe is actually us being triggered by that person. They are creating the reflection that we need in order to heal and evolve. For example if we come into contact with someone who appears to be very showy about their recent promotion, we may feel this person is arrogant and self-orientated. This, however, may not be the case.

It could be "cosmic scab picking" where the Universe is trying to bring your awareness to an unhealed wound that you are carrying. As an onlooker you may distaste for their "egotistical showing off". When this happens you need to get curious about why you feel that way. They may well be all of the above, but step back and ask yourself what the feelings are that you are experiencing underneath the blanket term of "distaste". Is it jealousy perhaps? Or resentment that you should have been offered the promotion?

Once you have been able to identify if this is a trigger, then the next step is for you to ask yourself what is underpinning this feeling and start to find the wound that you need to heal. Again, if you are not in a good place emotionally, psychologically, physically or energetically, it's going to be harder to read energy clearer and work out if what you are feeling is yours or not. This is where self-care and self- awareness are crucial, and even more so for those of us who have empathic traits.

Some humans are more sensitive to emotional energy than others, and they are known collectively as Empaths. This group of people have a heightened emotional sensitivity themselves, as well as being able to feel the emotions of others and the energy in spaces and places.

Discernment can be a challenge to Empaths, because they sometimes cannot easily identify where their feelings are coming from. Good self-care is a must for anyone with an empathic nature, and is the cornerstone that will help them to know how their feelings relate to people and occurrences around them (or not). Good basic energy housekeeping is helpful for all of us, but is especially important to Empaths. Morning and evening habits of clearing and protecting, good boundaries and becoming an expert on what drains them and fills them up. When an Empath is looking after themselves emotionally, energetically, psychologically and physically they can tap into amazing superpowers that they can trust and use for the greater good. (When they don't look after themselves they are prone to overwhelm, burn out, people pleasing and feeling like a basket case.) They are human lie detectors and can read energy in a moment and get a bang on insight into motives, falsehoods and intentions. Empaths are often found in the healing arts, and are the kind of people who you feel instantly comfortable with and want to pour your heart out to.

It is thought that their emotional body (one of the layers in your aura or energy body), is more porous than most people and therefore allows energy in more easily and quickly. This gives them the ability to read vibrations accurately but can also lead to energy overload if they do not clear it regularly.

Empaths usually need to work on boundaries. By nature they want to help others, and can be prone to stepping in and giving away energy that they really need to keep for themselves. If they are not engaging in good self-care, the likelihood is that they are feeling the emotions of other people on top of their own heightened feelings and this becomes unbearable.

There can be an accumulation effect that over time means that they become "peopled out" and need to withdraw for their own protection. This is often interpreted by those who don't understand as the Empath being moody or distant and sometimes even aloof. This is especially common for people who do not know that they are an Empath, and are trying to function in a regular job and life with no awareness that their emotional sensitivity is because they are different. People around them often label them as too sensitive, and this makes them feel like they don't fit into society and can be isolating.

Boundaries can feel uncomfortable, especially at first, for all of us. To an Empath they are very uncomfortable. Remember that they can feel the emotions of the person that they are trying to assert the boundary with, so they know that they feel disappointed, angry, upset with them and the Empath then feels responsible for the other person's "suffering". It is important for an Empath to know on a conscious level, that when boundaries are asserted you are actually helping the other person as well as yourself. Helping them in the sense that you are showing them how to treat you, and how fair exchange of energy works in friendships and relationships. Since Empaths are wired to help others, this is a really important reframe for them psychologically.

If boundaries are something that you have not had in place so far in your life then asserting them can make us afraid of how others will react to us. The truth of it is that if people around you have learned to treat you in a certain way, you have allowed it to happen – and now it's time to change that and educate them lovingly in a new way of being and relating to you, thus empowering you both.

A gentle way to start working with boundaries is to pre-frame the fact that you are going to be behaving differently, before you actually start. Say something like, "I'm going to start looking after myself and practice saying no a bit more, so if you notice me doing that please don't be offended or upset. It's not personal, it's just something that I need to do for myself and I might need some support." If this feels too staged then work out what feels right to you, and hold an intention that the perfect moment will arise for you to voice this in some way. Practice on safe people initially and get some wins. Once you've gently asserted yourself a few times with people you feel safe with, you will start to gather evidence that you can do this.

In my experience, the people who I really need to assert better boundaries with can end up being the most resistant to the new way of relating. Be prepared for this and refer back to your initial comment about this not being personal and that you are really grateful for their help, little and often and with love, keep reinforcing as best you can.

Be kind, but don't take on other people's reactions. Your intention may be misinterpreted initially, especially if you are changing the unspoken rules of a relationship where you have not been authentic for a period of time. Perhaps you have been a bit of a pushover and gone to social events that you felt uncomfortable attending, or maybe you've engaged in activities that you know you didn't want to but it was easier to go along with them and keep the peace. In truth, you don't need to justify how you feel to anyone. It's ok to say that something doesn't feel right to you at this time, and that is enough.

I am not saying that you have to have things your way all of the time, but neither am I saying that you should do things that don't feel right all of the time either. Real life is about balance, and the more you practice discernment and boundaries, the more you can get that balance right for you, or move towards it at least.

Compromise is necessary for harmony, and being able to balance this with discernment along with you love for others, and yourself is a key ingredient in happy relationships and life generally. When faced with something these days that feels like a poor fit for me, I tend to ask myself what the cost is likely to be for me. I look at this from two points of view - the cost of going through with the situation, and then the cost of not going through with it. I consider the time, energy and emotional cost to myself and others in both scenarios. I make decisions in as clear a space as I can, and be as conscious as possible. Sometimes it is less overall cost to go ahead with something than the cost of not doing it, even when it doesn't feel "right".

Buy yourself some breathing space – this is a great technique for you to adopt when you are working with boundaries and discernment. Making this your default position when you are asked for time, energy or attention will begin to relieve the decision making pressure in the moment, and allow you to step back and check in with the cost of a situation or request and how it actually makes you feel.

For example, a friend asks you to come over at the weekend because it's their birthday and they are having drinks and food – it wouldn't be the same without you! You're having a hard week yourself, your workload is bigger than usual and you've got some personal challenges going on at home that you are giving your time and energy to. You feel like you are starting with a cold and that's not surprising because you have been eating on the run at lunchtimes and most of it has been junk washed down with (more) coffee. Late nights and early starts are catching up and you seriously must hit this deadline on Friday at close of play or you'll be in it up to your neck. But you know from experience that they will talk you round, they'll tell you that you'll deserve a break by the weekend and that it will be fun. After all it's their birthday and you are their friend, so the subtext is that if you don't turn up then you are no kind of friend at all. (Side note – are they being a good friend to you in this moment?)

Usually you would fold, because it's easier to just say yes and get them off your back for now. By Friday you'll have this work done and you'll feel better – surely. But wait, you know in your heart that you'll need to schedule in some serious downtime this weekend and cave out with yourself because you are starting to feel overwhelmed. But how can you say no?

Here's the thing – you don't have to say no straightaway. For some people getting it out of the way is a huge relief if they can muster up the courage to pull up the drawbridge and outright say that they are not coming. For others it's easier to create some space where you don't feel pressured and you can look objectively at the cost from both sides. Buy some breathing space for yourself. In the moment when you are being asked to go, instead of saying no say something that is non- committal but will buy you some time and space.

- "I'll have to get back to you on that."
- "I'll see what's happening this weekend and let you know."

- "Let me see if there's anything else planned."
- "I'll have to let you know later I am juggling stuff here at the moment."

Whatever feels natural to you can become your new default position, and then you can free yourself from making decisions under pressure.

A note on Spiritual Discernment. In my experience this is becoming more and more necessary as we evolve towards a more enlightened way of living. Not everyone that sets themselves up as being a teacher, leader or healer in this area is a person who will serve you well to connect with, or to work alongside. I am a great believer in you trusting the way that you feel, but sometimes when we are going through a life lesson or challenging time, we can be vulnerable to making decisions that may not be in our best interest.

So many broken healers are not doing their own work. Their wounds and old story are so entrenched and deep that they are unable to evolve, and their life often reflects this. I feel that our modern-day culture of social media and instant internet credibility can fuel a public image that is actually a far cry from the reality of that person's life and intention.

People are showing up telling you that they hold the keys or knowledge to your hopes and dreams, when they haven't got their own life on the rails. No one is perfect and we are all a work in progress, but you simply cannot teach someone something that you know nothing about. Look for the genuine people, and look past what you see.

Many believe that they are genuine, but they are deluded and living in ego. I know of broken healers who are stepping into the arena as Law of Attraction teachers, when they are living in poverty consciousness. I know of so-called Spiritual Leaders who encourage drama in closed Facebook groups and manipulate an audience into staying because of fear, so that they can have their ego stroked by how many "followers" they have. I also know that in both of these cases (and far more that I could reference) that these people have no idea they are doing this. They are living in delusion because in truth they have not yet evolved past this. This does not make them bad people, but it does make them incongruent and perhaps a poor choice to work with until they have evolved further on their journey.

Do your homework, and make sure your BS detector is in full working order. Exercise discernment with who you listen to, follow or work with. And always know that you are your own expert. Take what you need and only that.

How can I support myself to make better choices of where I spend my time and energy and with whom?

What am I doing in my life right now that I can change and exercise discernment in?

Where do I need better boundaries in my life or relationships?

"I AM safe and free to exercise the power of choice over all parts of my life. I honour and respect myself by having discernment. I spend my precious time and energy with people and in situations that are in alignment with my greater good and who I AM."

LESSON 16

Heal your wounds

I AM *healing from my past because I deserve to feel good in my present.*

Lesson 16
Healing ~ Heal Your Wounds

~ You already know the truth. Now you just have to get your human self to allow it in ~
Sarah Dawn Smidt

Life is full of lessons, people and experiences that can hurt us. Past events can be contaminated with feelings of shame, guilt, desperation, betrayal, failure, anger, unforgiveness, resentment and more. Wounds from life can run very deep. Relationship break-ups, financial stress, illness, loss, family issues and anything else that's affected us in a detrimental way will have wounded us at some level.

These wounds are then filled with associated feelings and perceptions about "what happened" from a version of ourselves that is struggling and in pain. Life moves on and on a superficial level we may move on too, away from the invisible but unhealed past – but unprocessed and unhealed feelings fester, and they steal energy, joy and presence from us on a daily basis.

Now and then something might remind us of the past, or pick at the scab in some way. The undercurrent that we've ignored or tried to swim away from shows itself again in the cold light of day and we feel the surge of negative emotions that are connected to the past. The past has gone, but unhealed its residue remains and colours the now. This changes how you feel and lowers your vibration and energy in the present – and as we know through The Law of Attraction this affects what we draw in as co-creators for our future. Sometimes it's hard to even admit if we are wounded. We may have buried feelings deep because they were so difficult to deal with, and perhaps even subconsciously disassociated with them, banishing them into our own Shadow.

These wounds may become evident in situations where we feel pressured or stressed, emotionally vulnerable or when our inhibitions are lowered – for example, when we drink alcohol and become less reserved, and our vibration is lowered so we are more likely to align with the old negative feelings that are hiding within our wounds.

Identifying your wounds is the first step towards healing them, and it is a great act of self-love. Many of us don't want to go there because the past was traumatic and we don't want the old feelings to resurface, because they come with a cost. But what is the cost to you of not processing and healing these feelings? What is the cost of living a half-life where you can't be fully present without the pain of the past lingering in the corners of your heart and mind? What is the cost of the perpetual subtext in your life of feeling unworthy, unattractive or financially disadvantaged?

These wounds may only show themselves when someone around you experiences success. Your neighbour gets a new car, when a colleague books the holiday of a lifetime, or when someone walks past you looking attractive and happy with a handsome man on their arm. You feel the sting of jealousy, of resentment and of poor me. Your inner victim gets her pom-poms out and starts to party. You may have no idea where these feelings are coming from or what's triggered them, but you know they make you mighty uncomfortable and you feel in that moment that life isn't fair on you. The Universe just showed you that you are wounded – did you notice?

When the Universe picks at a scab to show you the wound underneath, there's work to be done.

Breathe, step back and be conscious. Get behind your response, and ask yourself what the deeper feeling is. (Jealousy, for example, comes from a deep feeling of lack or not being good enough. Ask yourself what has happened in your life in the past to make you feel this way.) Go back safely to key events that started the feelings in the first place, and from an objective and now time perspective, begin to observe. Have compassion for yourself. Perhaps you acted in ways that did not serve you in the past, and you can see this now in your more evolved state. Welcome to the human condition - when you know better you can do better, and that goes for all of us.

Maybe in the past, fear or emotional payoffs were so big back then that they highly influenced you. Perhaps you were blinded by love, poor self-worth or programming that you'd picked up along the way. It's pointless and unhelpful to beat yourself up about the past. It is what it is - and it's how it's affecting you now that you have power over. Name it, claim it and do what it takes.

If you don't heal your wounds, they will change who you are. You'll get stuck in a subtext of "what happened" and the feeling and vibrations associated with your perception of that (side note – examine these perceptions from your current more evolved self and with an overall belief that everyone is always doing their best, your initial perceptions were likely formed at a time when you were very hurt and could have been endorsed / encouraged by people around you who were observing the situation from an unconscious perspective). These feelings will contaminate your life in the present and send out resistance to manifesting good things in the future.

Doing what it takes to heal may look different to different people. There are two things that you really must do at this point, work out what feels right to you, and take action towards that. What happened in the past may not have been your fault, but it is entirely your responsibility to heal your wounds, no one else can do this for you. Avoiding the process because you are in fear of what it might bring up, that's not a reason to avoid it.

Depending on what you are processing and healing, you may need support from a professional, or you may need time, space and insight to do some deep inner work alone. If it feels right to you, revisit the Shadow Work chapter.

It's time to stop blaming others for the way that you feel and the way that things turned out. You may well have been dealt a hand from life that was horrendously unfair, and shit might have happened to you that would derail the most positive person on the planet. You might have been mangled, brought to your knees literally or metaphorically.

You may have been low enough to contemplate suicide (and if you are in that place right now you simply MUST reach out for help, right now – see this as a sign to close this book and make the call). If it's you I am speaking to, my friend, then I am sending you all of the love and support that I can muster up – and I hope you can feel it.

Whatever has happened, it's time to rise up. And for some of us that might be simply getting out of bed today and showing up. It could be starting to journal out your feelings, looking for the wounds and telling yourself that you are no longer held hostage by your history. It might be finding a therapist or confiding for the first time ever on a phone helpline that you need support. It might be putting down the bottle, looking at your finances, starting a diet or leaving a toxic situation. Whatever it is to you, know that you are more than worthy of a life that brings you peace and joy, safety and love. It's time to start healing and start living again.

I want to mention something now that I call my Missing Piece theory. Sometimes you feel such a level of unworthiness in your life that you feel unable to show up as yourself. The wound that you are carrying is one of "not good enough" and as with many wounds, you are unaware of its existence and the way that it is driving your behaviour and choices.

I first noticed this in myself. However, I didn't notice it until I had begun my own healing. I went through a time in my life when I felt horrendously unworthy, this was in the main due to a toxic relationship that eroded my self-esteem over the period of about ten years. (My more evolved self can look back now and see that I chose to stay in these circumstances and in fact contributed hugely to the contamination, victim mentality and general unconscious destruction of who I was. I've worked on the feelings of guilt and shame I was carrying about that time, and I'm way more objective and compassionate with myself now.) I was missing a huge piece of myself back then, and the gaping wound that this piece had left drove me to feel unworthy and less than everyone else. I unconsciously began to fill this missing piece up with anything that I perceived would make me more worthy.

I bragged about money and material possessions whenever I could. I one-upped people by showing off in ways that would make me seem more successful, and them less so (irony – it only made me look foolish.) I tried to fill the missing piece with what I thought was love, and I became a doormat to someone who used me, and I guess in many ways I used them too in order to feel significant and loved, even though in truth I wasn't either.

That version of me attracted in people and situations that were a perfect match to the mixed up and wounded girl I'd become, and it took a huge cosmic kick up the backside to get me to take action towards changing it. You may see a version of yourself in me. I see people filling their missing piece with food, alcohol, money, sex, cars, designer shoes and bags, holidays and more. Sadly in the era of social media, much of this is also very public, and sadder still the fix is temporary.

It sounds corny and done to death but I'm telling you that this is the biggest truth bomb that you will ever hear this side of heaven - the only way to feel better and really heal yourself is to go within and do the work. Find the wounds, name them and claim them and do what it takes to heal them.

What you are going to need is not in a department store, car showroom or for sale online. You are all that you need. Trust that you will know what to do, what to read or who you might want to seek support from. And for the love of yourself take some action.

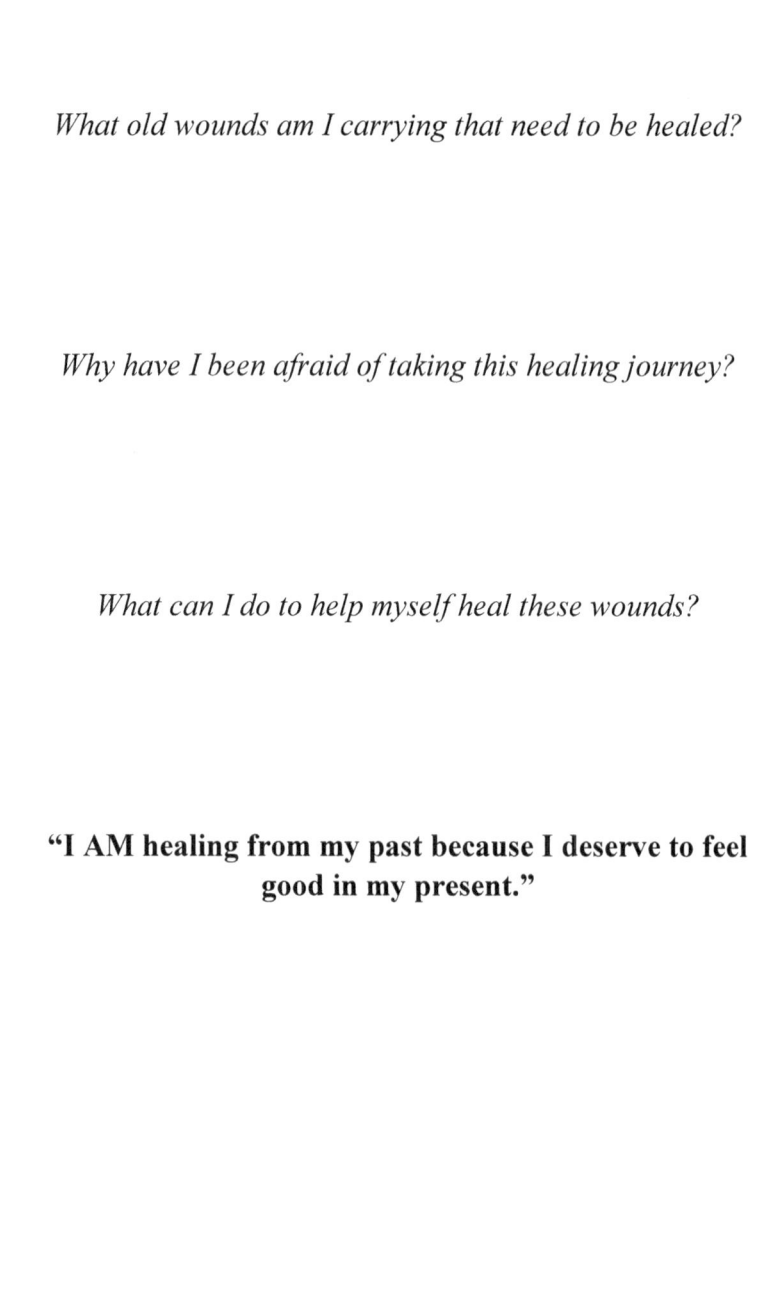

What old wounds am I carrying that need to be healed?

Why have I been afraid of taking this healing journey?

What can I do to help myself heal these wounds?

"I AM healing from my past because I deserve to feel good in my present."

LESSON 17

Ditch the drama

I AM living a peaceful life that is full of joy, abundance, love and happiness.

Lesson 17
Drama Queen ~ Ditch the Drama

~ Pour yourself a drink, put on some lipstick and pull yourself together ~ Liz Taylor

We all go through life events where we seek the support of others. This is not only normal it's also healthy. Someone else's perspective at the right time can help you hugely, especially if that person is conscious and coming from a place of love and objectivity. You have probably both needed a person like this at times, and been this person too. In most humans there is an inherent compassion that makes us want to stop or reduce the suffering of others, and when we see people in distress we want to help. But what about the people who seem permanently entrenched in situations that do not serve them? The people who always have some kind of crisis happening?

When one situation begins to resolve, another comes along replacing the first and maintaining that energy in their lives. How do we know if this is a life event that we need to be supportive of and play the role of a good friend, or if it's simply their Drama?

People stuck in Drama are unconsciously seeking a pay-off for their ego and therefore they want to draw other people into it. (Compare this to someone who is going through their stuff and seeking some appropriate support at the right time, but is generally getting on with it and focused on positive progress.) Drama energy is about letting everyone know about it, and will often include a process of recruiting others, because without other people involved there can be no payoff.

So what do I mean by payoff, and am I being mean? The Drama seeker is wounded at a very deep level and they are often unaware of this. Their Drama behaviour is in order to temporarily band aid over their wounds and feel better for a moment. They feel broken at a very deep level and whatever it is that they feel they are lacking in themselves, will be what they seek to feel by creating Drama.

The wounds that they carry will drive the need at a subconscious level, and because of this there will be a common thread to their Drama until the initial wound is healed and they are no longer seeking what they feel is missing.

Their need is often so strong that they can manipulate us to have time together in order to get their payoff. This manipulation may come in the form of flattery; they say you are their rock, such a good friend and that you are one of the only people they can rely on. This is done to guilt trip you into being available when they want their payoff. Remember in situations like this that healthy relationships are built on fair exchange, ask yourself what you are getting in return for your time and energy?

Another form of manipulation is the Drama seeker saying that they are there for you in times of need, creating a situation where they can "support" you, but then giving you a small amount of attention initially and then using aspects of your situation to spring board the story towards their stuff (again). They will then hijack the conversation, make it all about them and get their payoff anyway.

The end of an interaction with a Drama seeker is usually about them being grateful to you for "being there" for them, along with an attempt to secure the next contact that will get them their next payoff. Not committing to this, and giving yourself an exit that you can draw on in the future is important here. It gives you the future space to consider whether you want to go ahead or not and what the cost is to you.

Being friends with a Drama seeker can be exhausting and can create a dilemma. They have created such a "poor me" persona that although we know that much of their situation is self-created and perpetuated, we feel sorry for them. Even thinking about withdrawing our valuable support makes us feel mean. But ask yourself this – are you being a good friend if you are facilitating their Drama?

By allowing this to continue you are accidently encouraging it and teaching them that this is the way your relationship works. You are supporting them in being entrenched in Drama, and this does not serve either one of you. You might be contributing to the energy of them staying stuck and not making progress. Also think about the subtext that your behaviour is sending to the Universe about your own time, energy and fair exchange with life. If you are putting yourself in situations that you know are going to rob you of these things then you are sending out a vibration that they don't matter, and you will start to get other experiences lining up with this.

Always keep in mind that the Drama seeker is asking you for support or advice, but that this is not what they want. They don't want it because they don't want to make progress. Progress would mean there was no Drama, or less Drama, and therefore no payoff. Even after a long phone call or time spent together in person, where you have given good conscious support and suggested direction, you will find the next time you see them that they have either actioned very little or nothing at all. Their situation is likely to be similar or exactly the same. They may well have Drama based reasons as to why they "couldn't" make progress, and will roll out the next episode of the story, leaving you drained again. This continues and you start to feel resentful of the energy you are giving with the intention of wanting to help them. You feel out of exchange. This lowers your vibration and is combined with the guilt tripping they are happy to sprinkle in your direction, and you get out of flow in your own life.

Vague booking is a classic sign that you are dealing with a Drama seeker. This is when they post a comment on social media that hints at how broken / sad / used they have been, but does not tell the whole story. It baits people on their friends list to comment on the post or message them for more information, thus opening the door for more Drama. It is an effective strategy because it draws in a lot of people quickly, who by the consistency of Law of Attraction are likely to love a bit of Drama themselves and whip it up even further. And here comes the payoff - the Drama seeker feels heard, significant, loved and in the right, and is showered with attention.

What can you do if you are connected to someone that you feel is stuck in Drama? Ask yourself if you have become an accidental facilitator. Understand that you have "taught" someone that they will get what they need as an ego payoff when they bring you their Drama, especially if you have been their audience many times. This is not their fault or yours, so don't get into the blame game. It's a pattern that has been established between you both, and the Drama seeker now has evidence banked that you will give them the payoff they need. When you know better, you can do better and this is a chance for you to help stop the cycle.

Always approach with an intention that this is for the highest good of all concerned, and that you are not fixing them or telling them what to do. Remember you are about to change the rules of engagement and they may be long established, so a change in the way you interact will come as a surprise. They are both wounded and unaware that they are wounded, and they are likely to be unaware of the Drama that they thrive on – seeing it as life simply happening.

They need love, compassion and understanding, and may not be ready to hear about their Drama. My advice is to listen once more and listen very carefully. Be really present with them, and when they ask you for advice or comment give it once and give it very clearly. Be objective, kind and gentle, and know that you can most definitely do this because it is, in effect, the last time that you will comment in depth on this subject. Then draw a mental boundary with the Drama seeker, and know that you have held space for them and given them the best of your time and attention in that moment. The next time they go into this same subject (and this could be in the same sitting), take a breath and dig deep. Set an intention that you are speaking with love and grace and find the words to let them know that they have been heard, but that you have already made your feelings clear. Something like, "Well you already know what I think about that." Then gently change the subject.

Depending on how entrenched the old pattern is between you and the Drama seeker, or how stuck they are or how desperate they want the payoff – you may well have to do this several times. Don't get frustrated, know that this took a while to get established and it could take some reinforcement of your new standpoint to break. Gradually the Drama seeker will learn that you are not a person they can rely on for their ego payoff and will move on to someone else, or in some circumstances actually start to work on their stuff and really make progress. You could also start to give them more of a payoff for their progress than their Drama, thus reinforcing a behaviour that serves both them and you in a better way than before.

If you know that you are sometimes prone to creating Drama, you need to start to become conscious of when you are creating it and why. Step back and ask yourself what the payoff is and why you feel you need it. Exercise honest observation and introspection and see what you can find in terms of wounds. Then do what you need to do to heal and to feel more whole, worthy, significant and loved in the now in other ways that serve you better, and don't include Drama.

Where in my life am I being sucked into my own drama or other people's?

What is the perceived payoff for this?

How can I help myself to ditch the drama in my life?

"I AM living a peaceful life that is full of joy, abundance, love and happiness."

"Drama doesn't just walk into your life.
You create it, invite it or hang out with it."

~ Unknown

LESSON 18

Put down what is heavy

I AM releasing my own burdens and the need to carry others for them.

Lesson 18
Put Down What is Heavy

~ Let go or be dragged ~ Zen Proverb

We know the only time is now and that our power is in the present moment, but as humans we still drag around our history, our old story and our wounds. Resistance to processing, healing and resolving our past means that the load we carry can be energetically, emotionally and psychologically heavy and this can have a bearing on our physical health as well. We don't want to look at the past for lots of reasons, perhaps we are in fear that we won't be able to cope with unleashing old repressed emotions, maybe our ego wants to hang on to the old story of what happened, we don't feel like we've got the energy, we don't see the point, we don't have the tools or maybe we feel unworthy of moving forwards.

Whatever the reason, it's harmful on many levels to keep dragging our old stuff around, and an easy way to explain it and bring some humour to the subject is the metaphor of The Shit Cart! Some are lighter than others, and some are cleared out regularly. Some have stuff piled up so high that we are carrying a whole lifetime's worth of heavy, unresolved energy around with us that's stopping us making progress, slowing us down and even dragging us backwards. We add to this daily when someone hurts or angers us, a situation gets us down or we feel negative emotion that we don't let go of. This makes the load even heavier, and still we drag it up the hill called life. When it's full and heavy, even a small addition to the Shit Cart can feel huge. The combined weight of all that we drag around is often exhausting – emotionally, psychologically, energetically and spiritually. It metaphorically and literally weighs us down in so many ways. Some burdens weigh more than others. This is the Big Shit that we have not yet dealt with, and healing this will make the biggest difference to our lives and to the people around us.

But we don't want to go there, we don't want to look at it or dig. Because it feels shitty. But through Law of Attraction we end up attracting more shit into our lives if we don't deal with what's in the cart, and then we have even more to drag. If this is resonating with you there are two main things to action.

Firstly, stop putting stuff in there. Learn some tools, skills and techniques to stop adding to the load. You are more evolved now in your life than you ever have been, simply by being a passenger and gathering experience, learning and growing into your humanity. You know better now than you did, even just yesterday, and you will continue to evolve as time goes on.

Make a conscious decision that you are not going to put any more in your cart and drag it around, that you'll find ways to process as you go through life in positive and healthy ways as best you can. Hold yourself to this standard and practice letting things go, know that we are all doing the best we can and that it's healthy to forgive yourself and others. Cut cords, make burn lists, pray to whoever you believe in and stop accumulating more. From this day forwards stop adding to the pile.

Secondly, be brave and do what you can to sort your shit out. Making a conscious decision will help the Universe to start drawing in energy, people and opportunities that will support you to look at what you need to let go of and then help with that letting go. Get some books about how to heal from whatever your stuff is, see a therapist or hit up YouTube for some impartial advice and signposting.

Remember that you know you better than anyone else, and that you can trust your gut feeling when it comes to you healing and helping yourself here. Action is often the missing piece of the jigsaw, and I urge you as a gift to yourself and those you love, take some steps towards helping yourself if you know deep in your heart that you need to.

Something else that we can tend to do is to help other people drag their Shit Cart. This is of course well meaning, and as the big-hearted and lovely people that we are, we really want to help others but we can end up inadvertently harming both them and ourselves. We hitch their cart to the back of our own and set off again up the hill called life, dragging not only our stuff but theirs too. This stops them from carrying their own responsibility and adds to our load too. Ultimately this can lead to resentment from us as we feel out of exchange and don't see them making progress for themselves, when in fact we may well be stopping this by not allowing them to get on with sorting out their own cart.

You may need to help someone in a temporary way if they really need it, but as an ongoing measure it is far better for you to cheer them on from the side lines and encourage them to sort out their own stuff. Loan them your pump for their tyres, give them your map and encourage them on their own journey to healing and consciousness.

Think of yourself as both the signpost and also as the example. Refer them to books that might help, have a conscious conversation or introduce them to a therapy that you would recommend. Empower them to make their own progress and get on with cleaning out your own cart, and then you can shine as an inspiration and lighten your load at the same time.

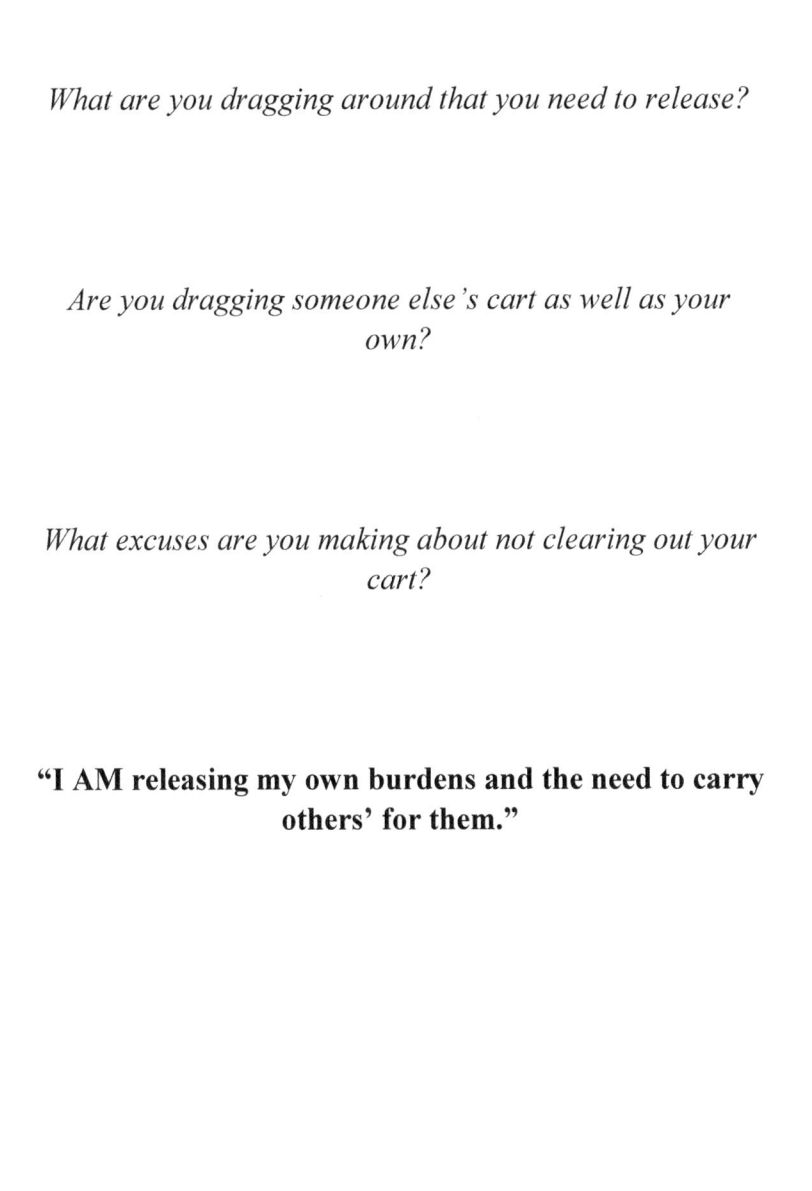

What are you dragging around that you need to release?

Are you dragging someone else's cart as well as your own?

What excuses are you making about not clearing out your cart?

"I AM releasing my own burdens and the need to carry others' for them."

"Dear Karma, I have a list of the people you missed."

~ Unknown

LESSON 19

Protect yourself

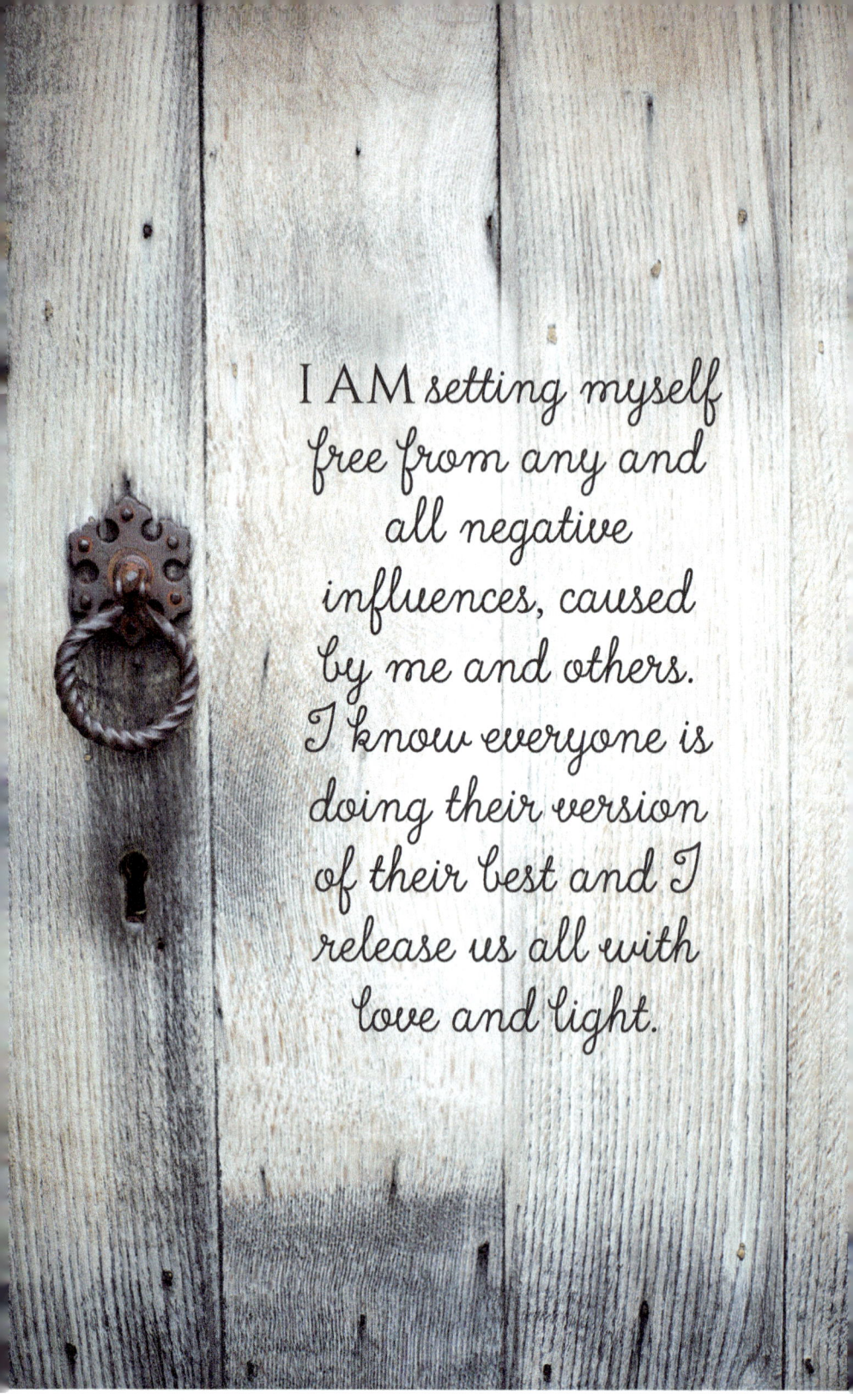

I AM setting myself free from any and all negative influences, caused by me and others. I know everyone is doing their version of their best and I release us all with love and light.

Lesson 19
Protect Yourself

~ Fools take a knife and stab people in the back. The wise take a knife, cut the cord and free themselves from the fools ~ Unknown

Everything is energy, and that includes our thoughts and intentions. Being responsible with your energy works both ways, protecting yourself whilst also being conscious of what you are sending out. As lightworkers and people of consciousness, we've often learned about energy, healed some of our wounds and begun to shore up a stronger frequency. We are powerful, and with this power comes responsibility.

I'm presuming you are like me, and that you would never intentionally harm anyone. But sometimes in life we meet people that tick us off, upset us or cause us trauma and hurt. In the aftermath we might wish that life would send them a whole load of "what they deserve". These thoughts are loaded with low vibration emotions such as hate, jealousy, contempt and resentment, and that travels from you to them. This builds a cord, and it is harmful both ways. They may well pick up on the energy that's coming their way and feel out of sorts, experience bad luck and more issues, which I will go into later. You can harm yourself by staying stuck in the negative feelings that are not serving you. The Law of Attraction will send you back what you send out – do you really want a version of that coming back anytime soon? It's important to be conscious of what you are radiating energetically, and also to process situations quickly in order to heal, therefore changing your perception of what has happened and the vibe you are sending out about it.

"But they deserve it" your ego might say at this point. I've been there and I can tell you that it's exhausting to be the Cosmic Police. Leave that to the Universe and settle with the fact that Law of Attraction is working for everyone, all of the time. You don't have to wish back what someone sent out, they are going to get it back anyway at the right time for their own evolution, so let that one go.

Letting go isn't always easy, sometimes a ritual can be used to focus your energy and intention. Creating a safe space and writing a heartfelt letter to someone who you feel has wronged you or that you may have unfinished business with can be helpful. At the outset you can set the intention that this letter is not going to be read by anyone else and will finally be burned safely, in order to transmute, clear and resolve or at least to begin the process. Because this letter will not be read by anyone else you have given yourself permission to be honest and unfiltered, and this can be very cathartic.

The freezer technique is something else you can consider, if you feel attached to a person or situation in a way that is not serving you. The intention is that you are going to freeze someone's energy and / or influence out of your life, without causing any harm to them or you.

Write the person's name on a piece of paper and draw around it with a pen. A yellow pen is the best symbolically but it doesn't matter too much, your intention overrides everything else. It's super important that you hold an intention for the greatest good of everyone concerned. Don't do this if you cannot generate that feeling or at least get close. Never do anything like this whilst deliberately wishing harm on someone, Law of Attraction is always responding. Now place one hand on your heart chakra and the other over their name and do your best to open your heart. Say "I bind you with light" three times, then fold and place in a small plastic bag or container, fill with water and freeze.

Cutting Etheric Cords can help you to disconnect, release and move forwards. These are the energy cords that bind us to people, places and situations in the present or the past. They can run energy in one or both directions and be as thin and wispy as a hair or as thick as a rope. Cords often keep us tied energetically to people and things that we need to detach from, and they can leave us feeling drained. Cords can mean that you feel energy from other people.

Someone else's stuff can show up for you and you may find that you have their anxiety, their low self-worth or their anger. Feeling not quite yourself or experiencing emotions or symptoms that are very different from the way you usually feel can be a clue that you are corded. A lot of people think that it's mean to cut cords with people, but in energy terms and done with a loving intention, the process is necessary to keep your own energy clear, and part of working with energy in a responsible way.

If you really are worried about being nasty to someone by disconnecting yourself then you can do a general cord cutting with the intention that any cords which do not serve you are removed, and not just them specifically. I cut cords every night before I go to sleep as a matter of course so that I know I am keeping my energy as clear as possible. Ask that all parts of you are present, breathe and get in to your heart energy. Invoke the presence of Archangel Michael, simply by asking him to draw close to you now and support you in cutting cords that do not serve. Give him permission to work in your aura and use his sword of truth to cut and seal any cords that do not serve you across all time, space and dimension. You may feel or sense this process, breathe and relax for a few moments and know that this is happening. You may find that you yawn or sigh as the cords are released, or you may feel a sense of freedom or a wave of emotion. Know that all is well and allow the process.

After a few moments give thanks for what you have received and ask Archangel Michael to surround you in protective white light that will help to keep your energy clear and stop new cords from attaching. You can do this any time of day or night and in any situation, apply it to a meeting where someone is pulling you down, a divorce where you are held over a financial barrel, or even just your day to day life as you interact with people who might unintentionally cord you.

It is important to know that cords can reattach, so doing this a few times a week is very helpful. They are more likely to attach after an interaction with the person in question, or sometimes even just thinking or speaking about them. Cutting cords on old situations can help you move forwards from them and heal, and the process can help you to move forward in your life and make progress towards new situations. Cutting cords with a property that you want to sell can be effective when you want to move house, and on past challenges to set you free of their influence, or people that you may be picking up a negative vibe from.

What if someone is feeling that you have wronged them in some way? They may well be feeling angry or hateful towards you, which energetically translates into you being sent an energetic vibration that will affect you in a detrimental way. Even if you feel you have done nothing wrong, remember that their perception of what has occurred is driving their feelings towards you and this is creating the energy that is being sent your way.

Being on the receiving end of focussed low frequency energy is collectively called a Psychic Attack. Most people are totally unaware that they are subjecting you to this, they just know that they are hurt and that they blame you. They are entrenched in their own story about how you wronged them, and the more energy they spend on that, the stronger the energy they will send to you. When you are under Psychic Attack you can feel really out of balance. Common symptoms include:

- Nightmares
- Tired and depleted of energy
- Feeling watched
- Unexplained anxiety
- Feeling overwhelmed and emotional
- Inability to concentrate
- Unexplained physical or emotional symptoms

(You must take responsibility for yourself and seek medical guidance if you need to.) It's important to try not to go into fear, this lowers your vibration and will attract in more low vibration energy that you don't want. Remember that before you read this you had probably ticked off loads of people in your lifetime and survived to tell the tale. Try to shift your focus and not send the situation or the person in question any energy, this will create more cords between you. Cut cords between you, do a releasing ritual and shore up your vibration in general by doing things that make you happy and bring you joy.

Get the basics right like good sleep hygiene, plenty of water, time in nature, no drama and high vibration nutritious food. Carry protective and grounding crystals, do some daily guided meditation about releasing the past and bubble up energetically. Do what you can to wish the other party well, they may not be as conscious as you and they are going to get back a version of what they send out as we all do in due course.

Which people in my life from my past or present may have sent me energy that is affecting me in a negative way?

What can I do about this, being mindful that I don't want to attract more by wishing them harm?

Who have I wished harm on in the past or present that I need to cut cords with and wish well for now?

"I AM setting myself free from any and all negative influences, caused by me and others. I know everyone is doing their version of their best and I release us all with love and light."

"Promise me you'll always remember:
You're braver than you believe, and stronger than
you seem, and smarter than you think."

~ Christopher Robin to Pooh

LESSON 20

Love your body

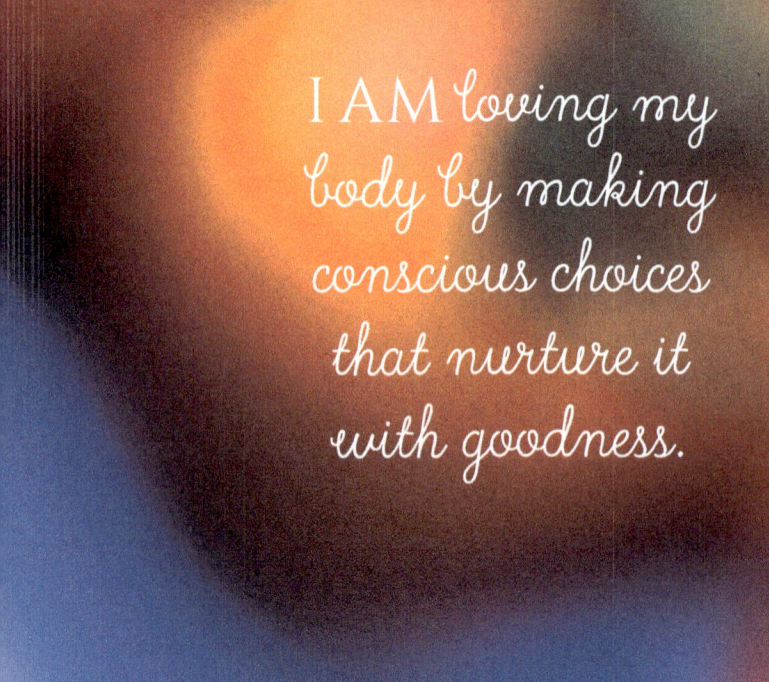

I AM *loving my body by making conscious choices that nurture it with goodness.*

Lesson 20
Physical Nurturing ~ Love Your Body

~ Take care of your body, it's the only place you have to live in ~ Jim Rohn

Our bodies are the house of our soul, and we have a responsibility to take care of them. Looking after your body is an act of self-love, and when we don't look after our bodies it is often due to a deep-rooted feeling of not being worthy. Think about it for a moment, if we truly loved ourselves and felt truly worthy then why would we treat our bodies in a way that we know does not serve us? Poor food choices, not enough water, depleted sleep, no exercise and self-reproaching thoughts, all have a harmful effect on our bodies.

We lead ourselves towards illness, rob ourselves of energy, vitality and wellbeing. None of us consciously want to create this for ourselves, so why do we do it? We are aware that it's happening, so why don't we stop it? Because we make excuses to ourselves that we don't have enough time, it's not actually that bad.

Healing your old wounds and starting to build up your own self-worth will help you hugely in looking after your body. Being conscious of the decisions you make on a day to day basis, stepping back and asking yourself "does this serve me?" will create a moment in time and space where you can change habits and make better choices.

Take responsibility and find out what could work for you. It's no big secret that processed food, too much alcohol and not enough water are unhealthy choices. In my experience, when I eat a plant based diet and cut out meat and dairy, I feel like I have a lot more energy and I generally function better.

There is evidence to support that this is a healthy way to eat and can ward off illness, and help as part of a recovery plan if you have been unwell. Empower yourself and exercise due diligence, and once you have worked out what you feel will be good to support your own health and wellbeing, get a plan and get started!

Even small improvements such as drinking more water can have massive benefits to the way you feel and function. The way you think and feel about your body also has an effect on it. Remember that thoughts are energetic, and thoughts that you repeat over and over become affirmations and start to attract in the outcome that you are focussed on. For example, telling yourself that you are fat is never going to make you lose weight, and telling yourself that you are tired will never give you more energy. Be conscious about the thoughts that you are sending to your body and make sure that they are thoughts of health, wellbeing and love. Send gratitude to your senses, your organs and your spine, all parts of you that function as a unit in order for you to be here in the physical.

As physical beings we were made to move. Exercise is important for a whole raft of reasons and can help to keep you healthy emotionally, psychologically and spiritually as well as helping you in a physical sense. Exercise doesn't have to be going to a gym and pumping iron, but if that's your thing then go for it. It can be gentle stretching when you first wake up and a brisk walk at lunchtime. If you really don't want to move then incentivise yourself by downloading an inspiring podcast to listen to while you walk. Walking is hugely under rated as exercise and has the benefits of being free, outdoors and can be done mostly anywhere. I find walking great thinking time, and it gets me grounded. You can use affirmations as you walk and they can become more powerful as you move your body and feel the benefit of associating what you think with a feel good physical response. Walking can also be built up to any level you wish and the only equipment you need is suitable footwear.

As with everything, find out what feels right to you and take some action to get going, but don't underestimate the power of simply getting your trainers on and taking a walk. If you are in resistance about looking after your physical body, think for a moment about the people in your life that you love. Staying well for them is important. Perhaps you are a parent and your children rely on you. Maybe you are an adult but your ailing parents need your support. Think about your spouse or life partner and how the quality of their life might improve if you had more energy and looked after yourself more. This isn't something you are just doing for yourself, it's a gift for everyone in your life.

Enough good quality sleep every night is vital to your health and energy levels. Sleep deprivation has been known to be used as a way of torturing people, it affects you that badly! It's the way that we restore ourselves and charge ourselves up for the following day, and as so many of us know, poor quality or insufficient sleep can massively affect how you feel, function and show up. Studies show that adult humans need between 7 – 9 hours of sleep ideally, and many of us are getting a lot less. So many of us stay up past bedtime to watch television, eat too late to relax and wind down, drink too much caffeine in the late afternoon and evening and sit using technology until the moment our head hits the pillow. None of this is conducive to a good night's sleep and will rob you and those around you of the best version of you showing up the next day.

Making a commitment to yourself to improve your sleep can bring about massive changes in your life, it can improve your performance at work and therefore career opportunities and earning potential. It can help you to show up in a more present and joyful way in relationships and will also support you towards physical body wellness, emotional resilience and psychological stability. If you are not getting enough sleep, or enough good quality sleep, then maybe it's time to see how you could.

I want to take a moment to add a footnote about our health and the place for medical / pharmaceutical support versus holistic approaches. I personally believe that there is a place for both, and that seeking out professional and appropriate medical care is a responsible and necessary thing to do when you need it. It concerns me greatly when people call holistic therapies and approaches "alternative", because I think that there is simply no alternative for good medical advice when it's needed. I use the word complimentary, because I think we should be open to everything, and then choose what feels right to us after we've gathered up as much information from credible sources as possible.

When you start to become more conscious there may be the temptation to view the medical profession as unhelpful with their pharmaceutical recommendations, and this can mean that you explore a holistic route to wellness first. That's your call, but I would rather get all of the facts from every possible source, including my doctor, before I made decisions about my healing. Just because you go and see a doctor and have a consultation does not mean that you absolutely must go ahead with taking what they prescribe or doing what they suggest. But it does mean that you walk out there more informed and more empowered to weigh up and measure what might be right for you. This might be the point where you are thinking that your doctor isn't very good and doesn't know about the issues that you are going with – if that's the case take responsibility and see someone else, but see someone if you need to.

Reiki, essential oils, crystals, kinesiology and any other therapy will often help your healing, but if you've got a broken leg you are going to need a plaster cast, and no amount of pixies, unicorns and affirmations are going to help without it. There is no shame in needing to take medication to support you while you work on your stuff in other ways either, for example depression. You may choose to take a low dose anti-depressant under the guidance of your doctor if it's appropriate, whilst looking at ways in your life to engage in radical self-care, shore up your energy and have a weekly aromatherapy massage. This is a responsible and helpful way to combine medical and complimentary therapies, and will often result in faster progress and make you feel more empowered thus building emotional stability and self-worth.

As always, do what feels right for you, but make sure you get as much information as you can from different sources in order to make decisions in your best interest and from a place of power.

What am I doing that is harming my body?

What could I do to show my body more love?

What are the wounds that are making me feel unworthy of having a healthy and beautiful body and how can I heal them?

"I AM loving my body by making conscious choices that nurture it with goodness."

"Like wildflowers you must allow yourself to grow in all the places people thought you never would."

~ Lorde

LESSON 21

Believe in miracles

I AM easily attracting and experiencing miracles in my life, because I am worthy of them.

Lesson 21
Miracles ~ Believe in Miracles

~ I am realistic, I expect miracles ~
Dr Wayne Dyer

Like anything else in our lives, miracles can only manifest when we believe in them. When we are closed to receiving one or doubt their existence, we are sending out resistance to experiencing them. This resistance means that we never get to perceive one in our life, and this gives our ego evidence to reinforce the fact that they can't possibly be real or that they never happen to us. This creates a concrete belief that a miracle is not going to show up in our lives, no matter how badly we might need one, and a perpetuating cycle occurs which holds us firmly in resistance.

So how can you open up your life to miracles? You have to start believing that they exist, and they do, all around us in our everyday lives and in the Universe as a whole. You are a living, breathing miracle and so is the whole of creation. Start to look around you and find evidence of miracles so that you can start to get more into alignment with them. Take a walk in nature and really look around you. Look at your child and think about the moment of their conception and how they got their hair colour and personality. Watch the sunset or listen to some deeply soul stirring music or poetry.

Perhaps it's not that miracles don't exist, perhaps it's that you have been in resistance to noticing them until now. I like to deliberately look for evidence of miracles and healing, knowing that through Law of Attraction what I focus on will grow in my life. I immerse myself in resources that will feed me with more evidence, and love books and movies that give me this. I know that if I can align with the energy and possibility that miracles happen for other people that I will be affirming that I believe in their existence and expect that they are around me in every moment.

I love learning about someone's prayers being answered, an inexplicable turnaround in health, a visitation from an Angel or anything else that to our human mind and ego seems impossible. As I observe such happenings in the lives of others, I am programming myself to look for them in my own life, and that I'll start to attract them into my experience which will not only bring me joy but may well touch my life with a miracle or two as well.

What exactly constitutes a miracle? The cynical amongst us may argue that unless it's water being turned into wine before their eyes, or the blind being able to see again then it's not a miracle. I disagree, I think that experiencing a miracle is entirely subjective and if you think that a miracle has happened and you choose to perceive it that way – then it has. For some people it might be finding enough money in an old handbag to pay a bill that they couldn't otherwise afford, for someone else it could be going into remission from an illness. I once helped a friend, and against all of the odds, get to her sister's hospital bedside just as she passed over, with literally not a moment to spare. To me that was a miracle, and to her as well. It's easy to allow life and the human condition to harden us, discounting events as simply co-incidence, but what if there was a greater plan and miracles were a part of that?

Some may say that I am naïve and gullible, but I choose to believe that they are not only possible but will come my way when I need them. Step back from your mind and your ego when they whisper to you that miracles aren't real. Look for miracles in the everyday, observe and acknowledge them and affirm their existence. When you witness a miracle, send energy and focus to it and deliberate gratitude for what you have experienced. Foster a belief that your life is full of miracles and that you are attracting them every day, this will open you far more to the possibility of them showing up.

Where are you blocking miracles in your life?

How can you bring more miracles into your awareness?

Does part of you feel unworthy of a miracle, and how can you heal this?

"I AM easily attracting and experiencing miracles in my life, because I am worthy of them."

LESSON 22

Don't stay a victim

I AM stronger and wiser because of the life lessons I have lived and healed through. Life is always supporting me and I AM loved. I can release the past with peace in my heart.

Lesson 22
Don't Stay a Victim

~ Sometimes the person you would take a bullet for, ends up being the person behind the trigger ~
Taylor Swift

There are times in life when we all feel like a victim and it is totally justified. You may have been betrayed by a partner, lied to by a friend, stolen from, experienced online fraud or even something way worse. Feeling harmed and feeling helpless to stop that harm is a horrible place to be. As with any kind of trauma you need time, Space and support to process what has happened, and the subsequent emotions after the event.

How you feel is personal to you and you must honour your feelings and do what you need to in order to heal. It doesn't matter how long it took someone else, or if someone else has been through something "worse" than you and now they are on the up. Everyone's stuff is big stuff to them, and you are the expert on how you feel and what you have been through. It's patronising and unfair to tell people not to feel like a victim when life has kicked them hard, so this lesson is most certainly not about that.

It is, however, about not staying in that energy any longer than you need to. Initially it may form a cocoon around you which you need to hunker down in. But there will come a time when this no longer serves you, and with all the love in the world when that time comes, it's time to be honest with yourself and start to move forwards.

Recovery from the past means healing and moving through the range of emotions, in an appropriate time frame and way for us. Give yourself permission for this. Don't confuse this with being "negative" that we are told to avoid by some spiritual new-agers. You came here with a full spectrum of human emotions, processing them and allowing yourself time and space to do so is vital to be able to move forwards, and move forwards you will. You may need help and support from professionals to do this, if you have, for example, suffered a trauma that has left you with post-traumatic stress or if the pain from the past is something that you simply cannot resolve and release yourself. Again, give yourself permission.

It's smart to reach out if you need to, because feeling like a victim after the event is going to affect your present and your future in ways that will not serve you. What happened to you is likely to have been wholly unfair. And it's even more unfair that it might hold you hostage in your heart and mind.

I am not saying you feeling like a victim is your fault. If you are looking at the world through filters created by your past, then you may think that I am blaming you. That's coming from your wounds, beloved soul, and not from me. There comes a time when being stuck in the story of what happened to you is harming you. Your ego may tell you that you are not ready to move forwards yet. Only you know whether this is true or if it's an excuse that you are making because you are in fear. If it's true, then there is more work to be done. If it's not true, then it's time to see it as resistance. (You are an expert on you, and it's time to get honest. If you need to do more work on healing the past then do that. If you are in resistance to moving forwards then name it and claim it, so you can start to work with it.)

Resistance is a normal human thing to feel. It is the result of your ego wanting to keep you "safe" and this usually means locked into your old story and comfort zone. I am not belittling what you have been through when I use the term comfort zone, it's simply a term to describe the familiarity and predictability of your life right now. Even though things may be far from great for you, there is comfort in knowing how life works here, and the ego wants to help you maintain that. Better the devil you know. But when you know better, you can do better. When you've realised that it is in fact time to move out of the holding pattern that you've been in, you need to start by overcoming your resistance.

When resistance comes up, observe it from a detached perspective. It's going to show itself as excuses, reasons why you shouldn't, make you feel like people will judge you for changing who you are and a lot more. Don't get sucked into an internal conversation with your ego about why you can't or shouldn't, this is coming from an aspect of you, and it's not actually you. Remind yourself that resistance is normal whenever we try to create change, send love to the parts of you in fear and keep going. Know that you are not "in ego" right now, it's simply your ego doing its job to keep you "safe".

Be open to the fact that you may be receiving a payoff in your life for staying in the comfort zone. This is an uncomfortable concept to consider, because it makes it sound like we are choosing this. Payoffs happen subconsciously, so this is not the case. Ask yourself if people around you have lowered their expectations of how you show up or contribute? Do you get special privileges at work, home or socially because of your identity and story? Are you allowed to make excuses for poor behaviour or standards in your life? Do you receive more attention, significance or sympathy right now?

I'm not suggesting any of the above to patronise you or criticise you. I'm saying them to help you open your mind and see why you may have unintentionally stayed stuck in a life that does not serve you. Only you know the answers to these questions, and only you can break this cycle and demand more from yourself.

There may be fear about who you'll become if you heal, change and evolve into a different version of yourself. What if you emerge from this process as wiser, stronger and more healed? What if your whole life changes in positive and amazing ways as a result of this one decision? What if you can feel more joy and happiness than ever before? This brand new you has never walked the earth before, and perhaps they will bring you a whole lot closer to who you came here to be. Think of the possibilities and start to get really excited about that.

Living in the energy of feeling like a victim is never going to bring you the growth and expansion that you came here to claim. You're going to end up playing small, feeling like the odds are always stacked against you (and they will be, thanks to Law of Attraction) and staying in a victim vibe. The past has happened, no matter how unfair it was, it's done. And your power to make the rest of your life the best of your life is in your hands right now.

Find out what your resistance is and use it as fuel to motivate you to change by acknowledging it and making a commitment to get past it and move forwards. Examine your story about your past in a safe way, unpick what happened, and unpack your feelings about it. Then observe the events of the past from a present moment perspective, what did you feel then and what do you feel now?

Remember that we are all doing our best, including you. Sometimes when you observe the past from your more evolved now time perspective it's enough to start to change the way you feel. Know that every single step of the way that you are entirely worthy of this and that it's time to give yourself the gift of freedom and not stay stuck in the story of being a victim any longer.

Where in my life might I be stuck in a victim mindset?

What do I need to do to move out of feeling like a victim?

Who or what is stopping me from doing this?

"I AM stronger and wiser because of the life lessons I have lived through and healed through. Life is always supporting me and I AM loved. I can release the past with peace in my heart."

LESSON 23

Walk the path for you

I AM *walking the right path for me with grace and ease. I am exactly where I should be in any given moment.*

Lesson 23
Walk the Path for You

~ You are the Universe expressing itself as a human for a little while ~ Eckhart Tolle

I believe there is a Higher Consciousness, and if you are reading this it's likely that you do too. Call it God, Goddess, Buddha, Angels, Krishna, Infinite Intelligence, Universe or whatever fits with your belief system. To believe in something bigger than ourselves is also to believe in a purpose or a plan. When you are open to the idea that we are here because of something greater, we can't believe that our existence is an accident.

Life can't be some cosmic blip that's ended up with us all on this planet, in this time, space and moment that we call the present. There are too many questions, occurrences and experiences that we have collectively tapped into as a species that tell us that there's more than our physical world.

Stories of narrowly evading death and seeing beyond the veil, miracles occurring at the eleventh hour, a medium who can accurately channel someone who has passed away, spontaneous healing and more phenomena that we can't explain with our logical mind and tangible evidence – but that doesn't mean they are not real and valid.

What I am saying here is there is more to life than we know. We don't understand it all yet and we might never be able to. There is also more to you than you know. You are entirely unique, and you are evolving in every moment. Every wound you can heal, every person you forgive, every cord you cut, every epiphany you have and every single step you take consciously is creating who you are becoming. We don't know our future selves yet, but I do know that whatever version of you walks the earth at whatever time, there will be no one else the same as you ever.

Think about that for a moment, it's true and it's amazing. You and me. In all of our messy human glory. We made it here against the odds, the sperm that collided with the egg that started to divide and grew into us. The soul that integrated with human form and brought through unconditional love and wisdom to complete us. And here we are, at the perfect time and in the perfect place to grow into who we were meant to be. I don't believe that we can possibly be here by accident. In fact, I believe in the opposite. I think we are here on purpose, Divine Purpose, and we are all an aspect of a bigger whole.

I know it doesn't feel that way some days, our path so far may have taken us in directions that have made us forget our true essence. We get moulded into the people we are now by society, culture, choices, obligation, life events and expectations. The path we started out on has detoured and taken us in directions that we weren't expecting, and that we couldn't backtrack from. This then turns into the path of least resistance, and we end up walking through a life that is the easiest option for us at that time, we might not love it and we might know deep down that we're not serving ourselves, but this path pays the bills and avoids conflict, it's approved of by others around us and it's not really that bad. We fall into the trap of "settling" for what we've got. Worried that if we change direction and start to search for more, that we'll be considered greedy, ungrateful or arrogant. The subtext of "other people are worse off than you" rumbles through our culture thanks to old attitudes from generations before. This is a misuse of gratitude, skewed and loaded in a way to keep us playing small, delivered with good intention from people who were trapped in their comfort zones and knew no better.

Many of us are secretly dissatisfied with where our life has ended up, but we daren't admit it, not even to ourselves. The path that we have walked thus far has not brought us the joy and depth of experience that we thought we'd be able to live.

Dissatisfaction is an undercurrent that lives under the material facade of our lives. Reminding us that we've settled for less than what we wanted. We are scared to get real and look at our lives in truth. Scared to see the wrong turns, dead ends and one way streets we've walked that brought us here. Because seeing them would mean that we had to take some responsibility for the journey and its current outcome, for the wounds that aren't healed and the shit cart we are dragging.

You might be thinking "but it's not that bad." Listen up - not that bad is not the same as good. Only you know the quality of your life, your health, your relationships with other people and your creator. Get honest with yourself and stop saying that it's not that bad if it actually is. We've forgotten who we are and why we came here, and who we were meant to become. We medicate with the material. A temporary buzz or band aid that makes us feel worthy. But what's going on underneath the handbags and glad rags that made you feel better for a few moments?

What does the day ahead look like when you wake up with (another) hangover? Did you notice that the neighbour bought a better car than yours? The latest phone isn't the latest anymore. Or we check out with the television, alcohol, food, social media and more. Distractions that help us to stop feeling the subtext temporarily, that life has become shallow by choice. One detour or shortcut at a time that compounded and made up the whole journey.

Maybe the path we walked didn't take us in the direction that we had planned. Perhaps we are stuck on a roundabout and keep doing the same thing again and again, but we just can't change lanes and get off. But where has that person gone who we first spoke about? That person with their unique human form who got here against the odds and brought a whole load of awesome to share? You've begun to play small, and given up on who you came here to be. Settled, thinking that this is the only path that you can walk now. Fenced in by previous choices and on a fast track to a life that isn't what you signed up for. And you think there is no way back, no way of finding your own path again that will lead you back to who you were before life happened. But you're wrong.

There is a way back and it's paved with intention, healing and consciousness. And that's not woo woo BS by the way – if you've resonated so far with what I've said it's the truth bomb you need to change direction and get back to who you came here to be. Here's something to consider. What if the journey so far hasn't been a mistake at all? What if it's been a glorious detour to help you to learn, expand and grow, and now you have the chance to evolve past the wounds and the heartbreak, the disappointments and the making do and you can rise up from it all? What if your past was all a part of your plan, but so was this moment right now?

The Crossroads. They come along now and then in life, and they can help you to change direction in a heartbeat. It's time to look at the path you are walking with honesty and compassion for yourself. Are you playing small in your life? Have you sold out on yourself? Where could you raise your self-care standards? How could you help yourself to heal from your past? What could you do to nurture your body? What could you do to improve a relationship? Does your environment need improving? How could you connect more with your children? How could you access more joy and happiness?

What if the version of you that can heal and evolve, that the world has not seen yet, is the person that we really need to show up? Maybe a conscious conversation you are going to have in the future with a child from a disadvantaged background who has given up hope of an education will inspire and motivate them beyond belief, and they will go on to find a cure for cancer, or win The Nobel Peace Prize.

Is this farfetched? I have no idea, but I am open to possibilities and miracles so I'm putting that thought out there. You don't know the version of you that has risen up yet and made the decision to walk a different path, so you have no idea about who you really are in your truth. We are all a work in progress, and that work is never done, but there is always an opportunity to keep expanding our consciousness. When we get stuck in the drudgery of life and it grinds to a halt. That's when we forget who we really are. But remember, you are not here by accident. We are all a part of the whole, and every shift you can make in yourself is a gift to all of us collectively. Each conscious conversation, each example and each act of kindness counts. Sometimes the greatest act of kindness you can give to yourself and others is to change your course. You are worthy of more, but it's something that only you can claim for yourself.

I'm calling to you now from my heart to yours, to stand up for yourself and demand that you raise your own standards. Find out where you need to alter the course of your life and start walking the path for you. Shelve any self-talk from your ego that tries to stop you. Ask yourself how you could contribute to positive change in your relationships, health, finances, work and environment. What do these areas of your life look like right now, and what would they look like in an ideal world? What kind of action would you need to take to bridge the gap? And when are you going to do it?

Harness the power of the moment and ask yourself if there is anything you can do right now? I dare you. Tread the path you came here to walk. Find a way to breathe new life into your world, and take action. Know that you are the person that creates your life, choice by choice and step by step. It's time to meet a new version of yourself. And I think you are going to like what you see.

How can I align more with my soul path?

What might be preventing me from walking my path?

Is there any part of me that feels unworthy of walking my path, and how can I heal this?

"I AM walking the right path for me with grace and ease, I am exactly where I should be in any given moment."

"The smallest act of kindness is worth more than the grandest intention."

~ Oscar Wilde

LESSON 24

Your message to the world

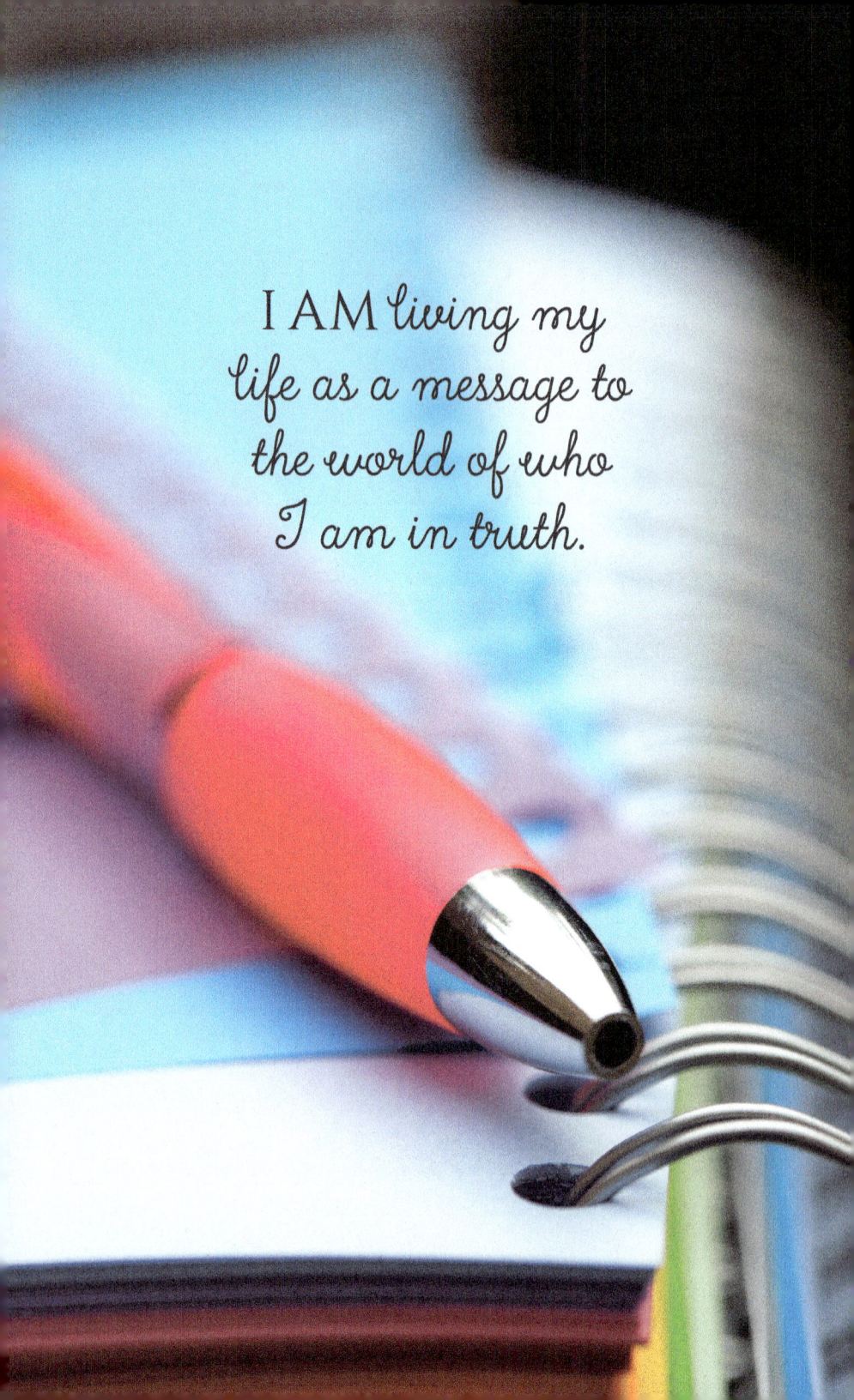

I AM living my life as a message to the world of who I am in truth.

Lesson 24
Messenger - Your Message to the World

~ Your life is your message to the world, make sure it's inspiring ~ Unknown

Just as you are entirely unique, so has been your journey through life. Each journey holds great value, and no two are the same. The wealth of wisdom that you carry is different to everyone else, and we rarely see its worth ourselves. What has become normal for you may be extraordinary to someone else and as you grow and heal, make sense of life's lessons and detours, forgive yourself and others, and step into your true sense of self – you can begin to share your message with others in ways that can help and support them.

Your ego may try to tell you at this point that you are not a messenger. That you have nothing of value to share or say, but I'm telling you now that this isn't true. No matter who you are, where you are from or where your journey has taken you, you have learned some things about yourself and about life. This is from your unique perspective, and will, as such, bring forth your unique insights and understanding. The more work you do on yourself to live consciously, the more sense these insights will make for you and the more you will be able to integrate them into your own mental map of reality.

You could find yourself in a situation where you have a conscious conversation with someone that changes the course of their life and you don't even know it.

Sometimes I receive emails from people that have resonated with a blog or social media post that has been exactly what they needed to hear in that moment. Until I read their email I had no idea that this was the case, and I am still unaware of anyone else that it may have helped.

You can still be a messenger without a blog, a website or a platform. We are all everyday messengers without us realising it. The way we live and behave sends information about who we are and what we believe into the world. The difference when you are on a path of consciousness and healing is that by default you become a more conscious messenger. The more we can evolve and live authentically, the more we can help other people with our examples, insights, love and behaviour. We are all in this together, all aspects of a bigger whole, and by helping other people to rise up, we help everyone else at the same time. You are probably doing this naturally already. A colleague will confide in you and you'll know which website to recommend.

You'll have a chance conscious conversation in the grocery store that triggers an epiphany for them. Your flight is delayed but it means that you can finish what you are reading and leave it in a café for the right person to pick it up next, and so they do and it makes the world of difference. Your child will show kindness to a boy or girl who was being bullied in the playground because you've explained to them that kindness costs nothing but means everything. You'll pick up a tin can from the pavement that someone has dropped and put it in the bin, the person that dropped it notices and becomes more aware of their actions. Perhaps you love to lift people up with compliments that are genuine and heartfelt. I know a gorgeous soul that writes love notes full of encouragement and leaves them on the train for the next passenger in her seat to find (yes Kelly McLean, I mean you) with the intention that they will end up with the right person at the right time and bring them what they need. The list goes on, and so does the message that you send out which sometimes reaches and helps people that you may never even know about.

Your journey has prepared you to be the conscious messenger you are. Look at what you have experienced and how you have grown. The learning you have benefitted from, and this may include the struggles that are still current in your life, and how you are working with them. When you know better you can do better. Part of doing better is holding the light up for others and shining the wisdom of our experience in their direction to help illuminate the path ahead. We are all messengers, so make the message of your life a good one. Because we can, and that is enough.

What can I bring to the world?

How can I share my message with the world?

Is there a part of me that is afraid of sharing my message and how can I heal this?

"I AM living my life as a message to the world of who I am in truth."

Summary of Lessons

Be Open to Possibility
Self-sabotage
You Attract What You Are
Old Stuff Keeps You Stuck
You are a Creator
The Law of Karma
The Law of Reflection
Compassion and Forgiveness
You Can't Fix Other People
Signs and Serendipity
Love Yourself
The Flow
Life & Soul Lessons
Being Present
Discernment
Heal Your Wounds
Ditch the Drama
Put Down What is Heavy
Protect Yourself
Love your Body
Miracles
Don't Stay a Victim
Walk the Path for You
Your Message to the World

"All you need is faith, trust and a little pixie dust."

~ Tinkerbell to Peter Pan

PRACTICAL MAGIC

"Honour your wonderful wise cosmically connected body. Trust the messages it gives you."

MAUREEN JOSEPHINE PROWSE
Mojolistic

Moon Cycle Magic

The energy of the moon affects us hugely; it has the power to literally turn the tide so it's no surprise that it can affect the human body and energy system. You can use the energy of the moon to help you to release what no longer serves you and manifest what it is you want to attract. Once you have an awareness of the moon's cycle you can use her energy to magnify your intentions in lots of ways.

New Moon – this is when we see from earth mainly the darkness, as the moon is illuminated from the back. This darkness is a metaphor for the new beginning that is about to start, and for the blank canvas that we have the ability to seed our desires and intentions for the cycle that follows.

You can use the energy between a New Moon and a Full Moon to help draw in and magnify your intention. Set a clear intention about what you want to draw in. Spend some time thinking about this and then write a list, remember that they need to be positive and in the present tense. You can supercharge this list by folding it and placing crystals on top, or putting it in a reiki box that you send energy to every day. You can ask for Angelic help, or any other help from the Universe that serves your highest good, but overall know that your intention and ability to align with the feelings that these experiences will bring are the most powerful ingredient.

If you want to have a New Moon ritual you can get centred and write your list with a candle burning and some incense filling the air, bringing any other aspects of spirituality into the mix that feel right for you such as drawing some oracle cards from a deck and asking for messages from your guides.

Once you have set your intentions remember to say thank you to the Universe in advance for the experiences that are unfolding for you. If you want to you can bury your list in the ground under the light of the New Moon, with the intention of the earth nurturing and energising your intentions to help them grow.

Full Moon – It is now that the moon is the brightest and it is when our emotions are mostly affected. This is a time when you can cleanse and supercharge crystals most effectively by placing them on a windowsill in the moonlight, or outdoors in contact with the earth.

Between now and the New Moon you are releasing. The Full Moon is the time that you will know what you have been able to draw in and manifest, or at least what you have been able to start to manifest. Celebrate small victories, the Universe hears this and sends you more. Say for example you were asking for financial abundance and you had a small unexpected windfall, it may not have been exactly what you wanted but you are still aligning with the flow.

Between now and the next new moon there is a time for releasing, this is an important part of manifesting what you want because not only does it make room in your life for more good stuff to come in, it helps you to stay mindful of how you may have been blocking your own flow and sabotaging yourself. You can start making a list of everything that you want to release including self-sabotage, negative thought forms, unloving thoughts and behaviours and more. Forgive yourself as you write your list and others that you may be harbouring bad feeling about, and know that when the time comes for the New Moon you can start over by burning this list. Make sure you do this safely of course, and call to the Violet Flame to blaze through all aspects of you and everything on your list in order to transmute lower vibration energy into high vibration love and light.

Surviving a Mercury Retrograde

The planet Mercury governs truth, communication, travel, technology and clear thinking. Several times a year it goes into retrograde (which means it passes the earth and appears to orbit backwards). It's not really going backwards of course, but all of the above may feel as if they are for you for the retrograde period, as unexplained and crazy things tend to happen to us all.

Trains and flights get cancelled, someone misses a crucial email that you sent, you can't get through on a number to make an urgent call… the mess that Mercury makes for us can make us feel like we are on the verge of a breakdown and that the cosmic odds are stacked so high against us that we will never again get out of first gear.

And to top it all off there is a phenomenon called a Retrograde Shadow, where typically two weeks before the stardust really hits the fan, you're already feeling it fly. So what (on earth) can you do to help yourself through this?

Firstly, know that it's going to happen and avoid (if you can) starting anything new in the way of projects and assignments. Look after technology, back things up and make sure that you are super clear on all communication, think before you speak and be conscious of any texts or emails that you send at this time.

Don't over commit in your schedule, there is going to be some wiggle room needed at times. Be super careful about signing anything that is legal or relates to contracts, check and double check or wait if you can until after retrograde to sign them.

Do what you can to chill out and expect delays, when they hit, reach for the book or e-reader in your bag that you thought ahead to bring. Double check all travel arrangements, passport expiry dates and reservations.

Don't take everything personally, wires are commonly crossed and tempers flare at this time. Be super clear when giving and receiving information, make sure you don't jump to conclusions and you know what others actually mean.

And finally - make sure that you turn up the patience and tolerance, we are all going through this but some people won't know, at least you have a heads up!

Crystals

Crystals are helpful little vibrational power houses that can assist us in healing, releasing and manifesting. They all emit an energy that is a pure and constant frequency, and these frequencies have been known to help us in specific ways. The frequency that a crystal emits will entrain your energy system to align with it after a while, thus moving you away from chaotic energy patterns that create an unbalancing in our energy as well as physical and emotional symptoms, blockages etc.

You can use crystals in your energy field by putting them in a pocket or wearing in jewellery, you can have them under your pillow or on your bedside, or placed around a room to help clear and lift energy. When you are choosing a crystal, it's a good idea to have some awareness of what that crystal may be useful for, but don't buy based on this alone. Take the time to hold the crystal and feel the energy of it, let your intuition guide you and buy what you feel connected to, not just what is says in a book or online. Have an overall belief that the exact right crystal will find you at the right time when you need it, and then trust what comes onto your radar.

You may find that after working with a crystal for a little while that you lose or misplace it. This could be the Universe passing it on to someone else that it needs to be with at the moment, or giving you an energetic break. Trust that this is happening in accordance with your highest good, and if it is lost hold the intention that whomever finds it will gain healing and positive benefits from it next.

Crystals absorb energy and therefore need to be cleansed regularly. You can do this by leaving them in the sunlight, the moonlight or running under water as long as they are not water soluble (selenite for example you can't). Once a month is usually about right but if you wear crystals this may need to be done more often.

I always like to test with a dowsing pendulum how much exposure I need to have to a crystal, with the intention that this is for my greatest and highest good. Never underestimate the power of these little gems, especially if you are energy sensitive. You may find you need to have a schedule to wear a pendant or bracelet, or that it's not appropriate to have a crystal under your pillow for more than a few nights.

You can also use crystals to grid a house, this will change the energy in the building and can help to raise the vibration and create a protective boundary around the property. Choose your crystals the usual way, by having some knowledge of what may be useful but also using your intuition. Using a dowsing pendulum can help you to see where you would need to place the crystals for the best possible outcome for all of the occupants. Beware of small children picking them up, a good way to avoid this is to plant them in a pot underneath a plant. This also lends the lovely earth energy to the crystal which they like to be immersed in, rather like going home for them.

Top 10 Crystals

Quartz – Amplifies energy, protects and brings extra energy to a person, room or situation.

Rose Quartz – Opens the heart chakra, facilitates self-love and helps love to blossom in relationships.

Amethyst – Known to reduce headaches, facilitate clear thinking and help you to open brow chakra.

Moonstone – Balances emotions and helps with intuition and fertility.

Haematite – Grounding and protective, helps overcome limitations and achieve goals.

Citrine – Energising and uplifting, associated with prosperity and abundance.

Selenite – Connects us with our guides, dispels negative energy and protects.

Black Tourmaline – Super protecting from other people's energy, electromagnetics and more.

Carnelian – Physical and metal energy, decision making, creative projects and career.

Flourite – Spiritual and Psychic Protection – helps to ward off any negative energies and keep your aura clear.

Space Clearing

Our environment has a huge influence on the way we feel, and since emotions are energetic, the space we are in can change our vibration in positive or negative ways.

Everything is made up of energy, and this is never more evident than a cluttered environment. When there are lots of things around you and they are all radiating a different frequency, this can feel very jarring and uncomfortable. Some people that are very energy sensitive may get overwhelmed and emotional, or suffer anxiety in this type of environment.

A good clear out is often enough to lift the energy in a space, and if you have difficulty in doing this here is an idea you can try. First of all, know that you are only committing a set period of time to this task, whether that is ten minutes, half an hour or more, you choose. Set a timer and find something to listen to that makes you feel good. Know that whatever happens next you are doing your best.

Commit to making three piles, one is to throw away, one is to pass on to charity or goodwill and the third is to keep. Start your timer and go for it!

See how much progress you make in the allotted time, and get some pace about it. When you move your body you change your state from stuck to taking action and the Universe hears this, you will feel your vibration lift – if not during this process, then definitely at the end. Quite often, people keep going long after the timer because they are enjoying the feeling of clearing out what does not serve them.

Do this with the intention that you are letting go of what you no longer need, in order to make room for new positive opportunities and experiences. Have gratitude for the items that you are passing on or throwing away for their service to you so far in life, and release them with love.

If you find yourself getting stuck, stop and ask yourself "does this serve me right now?" and if the answer is no, find the pile it belongs to. Even a little progress using this method will help you to change the energy in your home and make you feel better, which in turn lifts your vibration and helps you to manifest more of what you want.

Once you have decluttered, some quick and easy ways to raise the vibration even more are as follows:

- Clap your hands in each corner of the room.
- Use bells or tone into the corners.
- Introduce more earth energy with plants and crystals.
- Ask that the space is flooded with Angelic light.
- Visualise the Violet Flame blazing through the room to transmute energy.
- Smudge with sage stick.
- Burn essential oils and essences.

Chakras

Chakras are the energy centres that draw in universal energy from the world around us and move it through all layers of our aura, our meridian system, and into our physical bodies. The word chakra comes from the Sanskrit word "wheel" because of the round shape and constant motion of these structures. There are seven main chakras in our human energy system, and each corresponds to a different aspect or part of us.

They can become blocked because of past trauma, psychic attack or etheric cords from situations, places or people. When this happens you may experience symptoms related to that chakra in a physical, emotional, psychological or spiritual way depending on what is going on with you at the time. Here is a list of what each chakra relates to and some clues that will help you see if you are blocked in any way:

Crown Chakra – Top of Head - Violet

This relates to your connection to your higher self and All That Is. Think of it as cosmic broadband. This connects you to the Universe, your guides and to the creative energy that we call God / Goddess Creator / Divine Director. If this chakra is blocked it is likely that you may not feel connected to your higher self, you may struggle to tune into your intuition and perhaps be getting bogged down in earthly drama instead of stepping back and raising your vibration above it.

"I AM connected to my Higher Self and All That Is."
Crystals – Selenite & Clear Quartz
Essential Oils – Lavender & Frankincense

Brow Chakra – Forehead – Indigo

This is the chakra of multidimensional awareness and perception, whereby you can tune into people and situations in a more sixth sensory way and work with your inner knowing and psychic abilities. Many of us close this down because we are fearful of what we might "see". Have an overall intention that you are only going to see or experience what is right for you at this time and in your highest good. Then you can release any fear knowing that you will not be able to access anything that could bring you harm. Remember that people tune into information in different ways, just because you do not vividly "see" does not mean that you are not receiving sixth sensory information. You may experience a knowing, or a feeling or even hear messages and insights. However information comes to you is right for you.

"I AM embracing my multidimensional awareness."
Crystals – Amethyst & Lapis Lazuli
Essential Oils – Juniper & Rosemary

Throat Chakra – Throat - Blue

This chakra is associated with authenticity and truth; it's about you being able to express your truth in your speech and in your behaviour. In other words be aligned with your real self, and show it. When this chakra becomes blocked, it is usually in situations where people are unable to be themselves or say how they feel.

This can manifest as a clearing of the throat or cough, recurring throat infections and such. Sometimes this can be selective depending on which company you are in, for example you may be totally fine with your friends but when you are in the presence of a particular family member or colleague you always have an issue with your throat because you are in fear of them judging you if you are your real self. This is also a chakra where anger and resentment become stored, especially when you do not have a change to voice it.

"I AM safe to express my truth with love and grace."
Crystals – Blue Kyanite & Sodalite
Essential Oils – Eucalyptus & Chamomile

Heart Chakra – Chest – Green

This chakra is associated with love for others and for yourself. It is often closed down as a result of being hurt emotionally, but this can have a tendency to trap the trauma and pain within the chakra and stop you from processing and releasing it. If the time is not right for you to do this and the situation feels too raw, first of all be gentle with yourself and know that this will happen at the perfect time. Secondly, do what you can to get into the vibration of gratitude. Notice what you can in your everyday life that you can be thankful for and even when you feel really hurt, send thanks to the Universe for the gifts in your life. This could be as simple as the food on your table, running water, your physical body, a sunny morning or a song on the radio. When you focus on what is good you can gently open your heart again with the intention of releasing those old wounds and healing at the right pace for you. Also look for ways that you can show yourself love and support yourself emotionally.

> "I AM love in human form, my life reflects love back to me."
> Crystals – Rose Quartz & Green Aventurine
> Essential Oils – Rose & Ylang Ylang

Solar Plexus Chakra – Bottom of Rib Cage – Yellow

This chakra is associated with self-worth, self-image and self-confidence. This is the chakra that becomes blocked when we feel less than, or unworthy in any way. It's the one where we feel anxiety and a wobble coming on when we don't feel good enough in a situation or a relationship. It is really common for issues to arise in this area when we have had a knock in life, or a relationship has been unconscious or toxic and robbed us of our self-esteem.

> "I AM worthy of all things good, simply for being me."
> Crystals – Citrine & Yellow Jasper
> Essential Oils – Black Pepper & Neroli

Sacral Chakra – Navel – Orange

This chakra is associated with sexuality and emotions and as such is commonly blocked or holding on to trauma from past relationships that have been challenging, toxic or unconscious especially if there has been sexual intimacy. There may be unprocessed feelings stuck in this energy centre that stop you from processing the relationship or its effect on you, and you may feel that there are wounds to heal around masculine and feminine issues and emotions. There could also be a pattern of emotional reactions because feelings have not been addressed and wounds are still raw.

"I AM emotionally healing and balancing in perfect time and order."
Crystals – Carnelian & Red Jasper
Essential Oils – Jasmine & Sandalwood

Base Chakra – Bottom of Spine – Red

This chakra is associated with us being grounded, present and connected to the earth. It is the chakra that gets blocked when we are fearful of being present on the earth and facing issues that are coming up for us, and is especially connected to money and flow. When we feel less than abundant this chakra stops its flow. It is also associated with the practicalities of living on earth and making sure that your basic needs are met such as food, shelter and warmth. If these are threatened in any way through a loss of income or a change in circumstances then this chakra is the one to close. This creates a huge issue because you can only work with Law of Attraction effectively if you are present, and when this chakra is blocked you cannot get grounded.

"I AM safe being present and grounded on the earth."
Crystals – Haematite & Black Tourmaline
Essential Oils – Geranium & Patchouli

Chakra Self-Healing

A simple and very powerful way to help your chakras to release stuck energy is to gather a crystal, an essential oil and the affirmation that you need for that chakra. Get grounded by visualising your light cord travelling from your base chakra, down your legs and into the earth, ask that you are fully anchored and connected. Draw this energy up (simply through intention, don't worry if you don't feel anything) through your chakras and out of your crown, asking to be connected to All That Is. Now ask that all parts of you come in to the now time in order to receive this healing energy and to release old stuck wounds, lower vibration energy and anything that does not serve you.

Hold the crystal over the chakra in question with one hand and in the other hold the essential oil. Breathe in the scent of the oil and "send" the vibration with your intention to the chakra you are working on. Exhale and blow down your chakra column to the earth whilst thinking or saying out loud the corresponding affirmation. Repeat this 3 – 7 times, you may feel a tingling in your body as old energy leaves, or a wave of emotion. Intend that the energy is sent to the earth for recycling and give thanks for the lessons you have learned and the release you now draw in. You may want to keep the affirmation in your awareness for a few days in order to help the release process and to help integration of new positive vibrations as they come into your life. You can write it down and pin to a pin board, carry it in your purse or pocket, or simply memorise and use throughout the day. Likewise you can carry the crystal with you and use the essential oil in a burner to help you process.

What's on the Cards?

I love Oracle Cards and find them a great tool to help me connect with my higher self and my guides, to bring me confirmation and to help me to stay on my soul path. I have nothing against Tarot, I simply prefer Oracle Cards as I find them easier to use and read.

When choosing a deck of cards, trust your intuition and see what is calling to you. There are so many different kinds out there that you will be able to find something to suit, whilst holding the intention (and perhaps checking with a dowsing pendulum) which deck will work best with you. Don't give up if you get a deck of cards that you feel don't suit you, it may be that someone you know is manifesting some cards and they came to you in order to pass on! This has happened to me at least twice, don't give up just find the cards a new home and look for some more.

Once you have your lovely cards and you are ready to start working with them, a good way of starting is to hold each card in your left hand and look at it for a moment. The left hand is for reading and receiving energy, so you can ask that you are connected with the intention for that card and the messages that it holds. I like to place the card over my heart chakra next and read the description in the accompanying book for that card. I let the energy settle for a moment, I look at the card again, and then I return it to the deck and choose another.

Initially, and perhaps over a period of days I do this with every card. Please note that this is not to memorise each card, you will always have the guidebook, and if you want to go on to read cards regularly you will find after a while you don't need it. This is simply to set a clear intention with the Universe that I am ready to work with the energy of these cards and the messages that they will impart to myself and others.

There are lots of different spreads that you can use, but I prefer to work intuitively and see how many cards I think I should draw at that time. You can do a card a day for yourself, or three cards at the beginning of the week for example, or a full six or twelve month spread. If in doubt I check with my pendulum and ask "how many cards do I need today?"

A word or warning, nothing is set in stone!

The Universe is in a state of constant change and flux, and when you draw cards for yourself or others or when you have a reading from someone else, they are tuning in to the energy that is around you now and reading likely future possibilities based on the present. So often people unconsciously adapt their lives to mirror the detail in a reading, and then believe that by default the rest of the reading must be accurate. This is not always the case and a great opportunity for you to exercise discernment and also your own intuitive insights.

Trust your gut feeling, and use cards as another tool to help you in your life, but know that you always have freewill and that nothing is really set in stone.

"Don't use your energy to worry.
Use your energy to believe."

~ Joel Osteen

THE ENERGY OF MONEY

"I believe that if you point your heart in the direction of your dreams, that the rest of you will follow and you'll create and allow what it is you want."

Emma Johnson
Inner Smile

Money

Money is the name of the energy exchange that we use on earth, and it's something that we as healers, light workers, empaths and sensitive souls can get tied up in knots about. But why do we feel so uncomfortable?

This can be for several reasons, but at the root of all of them lie our beliefs about money. We all have a "money story" based on what we have learned from our lives and our experiences, and this is what drives our behaviour as well as our point of attraction.

Inherited Patterns

What was your parents' relationship with money like? Perhaps you were brought up in an environment where there was financial struggle and hardship, and the discussions and attitudes to money that surrounded you reflected this.

Our beliefs are formed early in our lives, and as we find evidence to support them, these beliefs become stronger. Maybe some of what you saw and heard as you were growing up has made you fearful of not having enough money, or judgmental about people who are abundant. The thing to remember about our inherited patterns is that our parents lived in a completely different time and reality. What was relevant then may not be now, and if we try to navigate through our lives using the old beliefs that we have absorbed through our upbringing, we could be sabotaging our progress in a big way.

For example if your parents were financially challenged, they may have viewed people that had money as greedy or snobby. This idea would have been generated from the lack that they felt, and associated emotions such as resentment and maybe even shame. If you happen to have integrated that belief into your own frame of reference, then there could be a part of you right now that is pushing your own prosperity away because you don't want to come across as being greedy.

Likewise if your parents had to work incredibly hard for all that they had, it's likely that you have some money beliefs that in order to generate an income you have to work incredibly hard. This could set up behavioural patterns that sabotage parts of your life – for example, if you are so driven to work hard, you will miss out on family and friends, and work could well become your priority.

Another interesting thing about inherited beliefs is that often the person who imprints these beliefs onto you - in a well-meaning, this is how the world works kind of way - could well have had the same done to them in their formative years. They will be carrying around beliefs that their parents had been influential in creating, and then passed a version of these onto you, and of course the same will have happened to their parents and so on.

Many of the beliefs that you have may not be yours in the first place and may be so outdated that they are definitely not serving you in the world we live in now.

Cultural Concepts

A Mind Virus is a concept or an idea that catches on. Something that is spread from person to person quickly and accepted into their frame of reference before it's passed on again. Some Mind Viruses can be really useful such as the concept of recycling. When I was a kid I'm pretty sure that everything went in to one bin bag and there was no sorting paper, card, glass or metal to help the planet and ourselves. Now it's commonplace to see bins in public places that encourage you to separate rubbish, and we do it in our homes as well. Initially thought of by a person or group of people, this concept has now become the norm, and has spread globally. Local authorities caught on and businesses, the government gave incentives for recycling and so on. It's something we do, but it's also an example of a Mind Virus because as a concept it spread around a lot of people.

Other examples include Facebook, it's something that has caught on big style in our modern lives and most people that you connect with will either have an account or at the very least be aware that it exists. The latest fashion can be a Mind Virus (suddenly everyone I know has a Pug or the Pokemon Go app), it's any kind of concept that is passed from person to person and beds into your consciousness.

The very worst examples of concepts that have gripped humanity include the concepts associated with the Holocaust, which was started by one person's delusions of grandeur and hatred that combined with a position of power and influence and led to many people being influenced to do unspeakable harm to others. So what has this got to do with money?

The culture we are a part of in a broad sense, and the culture that we are a part of in terms of our social groups, will be influencing our money story. Think for a moment about how you see yourself in the world. Would you say you are doing well? Where would you say you were in a "class" system, if you believed one existed? How do you measure yourself against the rest of the world financially? And what beliefs have you absorbed about this along the way?

Examples of cultural beliefs about money may include the glass ceiling concept, women being paid less than men and the need to bolster up self-worth with designer merchandise. These beliefs are the ones that are created by the world we live in, the media and society in general. When you move even closer into your circle and the culture of your family and friends, you are likely to find that your money beliefs are in alignment with the people that you connect most with. We become like the people we spend time with, and our money beliefs are often no different.

If your money beliefs are very different to the people you are connected with in your circle of friends and family, it is likely that those you feel different to will irritate you when you talk about money. If you have healthy money beliefs you will find people with unhealthy beliefs very hard work and you may see them as being stingy, mean or self-sabotaging.

If you have unhealthy money beliefs you are going to find people in abundance as show-offs, who rub your nose in it and think they are better than you.

These examples are two opposing ends of the spectrum, but wherever you are on that scale you will find that whatever you think of other people and their money stuff is actually shining a light on your money stuff. The question is, now that you are aware of that are you going to do anything about changing it?

Your Attraction Field

Not only do limiting beliefs contribute to your day to day struggle in terms of money, they are also setting up the same pattern for the future. As long as you stay in your story of how things are with money, and how things should be, the more of the same experiences you will draw in. This will give you even more evidence that you are totally right, and your ego will love that kind of certainty.

"See? It's always been this way, and it always will be. People like me are never going to make it unless we win the lottery. And I don't want a big win mind, I don't want to be like those greedy buggers over the road with their new car every three years and their holidays abroad."

And so the pattern perpetuates, and so you get even more evidence, and so you stay well and truly stuck in your story and therefore your experience, because Law of Attraction continues to send you a match to what you are sending out. And you are so entrenched in your story that you expect it more and more, and draw it in at a rate of knots.

Observing other people's financial progress makes you resentful and adopt an attitude of "It's alright for them." This contributes to a mindset of "poverty consciousness" that is going to keep you absolutely stuck. You might not recognise yourself entirely in this picture, but if there is a part of your financial experience that you want to change, then there's a part of your story that you have to rewrite. That process starts with identifying the beliefs that you have about money.

What's your Money Story?

Dig deep and think about your money beliefs. What has your upbringing and life experience taught you about money so far? What are the thoughts and feelings that you honestly have about money?

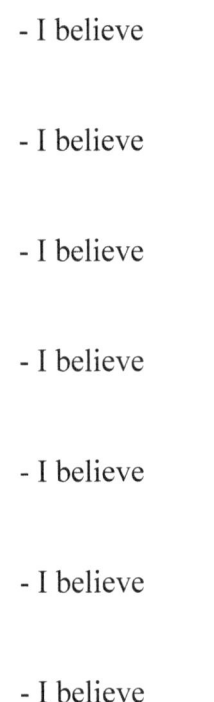

- I believe

- I believe

- I believe

- I believe

- I believe

- I believe

- I believe

Even the process of just writing these beliefs down might make you start to question them. Let's take that a little further, ask yourself the following questions:

Is this mine?
Is this true?
Does this serve me?

The answers are likely to be a resounding no if your money experience is causing you frustration or pain in your life. Beliefs are formed by us gathering evidence to support them. As we have seen, often this evidence is presented to us by well-meaning people in our lives such as family and friends, and also by the media and the world we live in.

We accept this evidence and use it to prop up our belief, because as long as we can justify it to ourselves we can experience something called congruence. When we work on changing our beliefs it can feel uncomfortable, because the evidence that we thought was relevant and correct, can actually turn out to be stuff that we haven't really thought about and we have accepted on face value.

We have used these snippets of evidence to build the foundations to solid beliefs that actually turn out to be nothing more than a house built on sand once you are brave and honest enough to dig. And often the sad part is that these beliefs have been the bedrock for our life experience thus far. An example for me would be that I had a belief that it was super important to go to university, get a degree and then a "proper job". That was the only way that I was going to make any real sustainable money to support myself and a family. This was both an inherited belief and a cultural one at the time, and there was plenty of evidence for me to lay the foundations. Many of the adults in my life that were doing well financially had followed this path, having a degree was a benchmark of ability in most professional positions and the media told me that people who had graduated got paid more and had better prospects.

All of this information supported the belief that this was what I had to do in order to create a life with financial stability and success. So I did it. I landed my "proper" job in pharmaceutical sales, and just as I'd been promised the abundance flooded in.

It was about four years into this career that life blessed me with the most glorious gift, and I became a mother. There was simply no way that I could return to the demands of the job I had previously thrived on, and I went into panic. My beliefs were all set up to help me to be the person that I used to be, and I had no evidence to support the fact that I could leave corporate life and still be financially stable. This was a huge turning point for me, I knew that I couldn't go back to doing the job that I had, but I was so entrenched in my "proper job" story that I couldn't see any way forward.

The result was huge emotional stress and upset for me, until I could let go of those "proper job" beliefs that were holding me hostage. Luckily I was open minded enough (or scared enough?) to entertain the possibility that there could, maybe, be another way. I started to look at ways that I could maybe stay at home and work part time, and I also began to subconsciously gather evidence to support the new belief that was emerging. In the past when my beliefs were first formed, it would have been ridiculous to think that anyone could run a business from home using the internet and social media to make a good income.

I had no evidence of this working for anyone in my social sphere of influence at all. I latched on to the nearest feeling example and used the evidence that I could draw on to build a new belief and a new story and to help me model successful behaviour. And the turning point believe it or not was EBay!

This was a community where I could see lots of people working from home, online and making good money. The evidence was right there in front of my eyes. If they could do it then so could I. This evidence was used to shore up a new belief and send me in another direction entirely, and a one that led me to where I am today.

So now when I look at the belief that says, "You can only make a financial success of yourself in a proper job" I find that the evidence is not there for me.

Is this mine? No.
Is this true? No.
Does this serve me? Hell no.

What new beliefs do you need to create and what evidence can you use to support them? (The new belief could well be the opposite of the old one.)

- I believe

My evidence is:

- I believe

My evidence is:

- I believe

My evidence is:

- I believe

My evidence is:

It's probably a good time to bring up the concept of Worthiness, because if you feel unworthy of receiving then these statements will be really hard for you to create. Here's the thing - there is an endless supply of money and energy out there, fact. Imagine someone attaching a hose pipe to a tap and turning the water on full force. That's the flow of money and energy that you have access to, but your old beliefs are the equivalent of you standing on the pipe and pinching off the flow. You are totally worthy of lifting your foot up and allowing more goodness to flood into your life. No matter who you are, what you have been through and what other people have said to you. No matter how deep the scars, or how much you have messed up.

Today is the day that you can start over and you do not have to prove that worthiness to anyone. You're here. That sperm met that egg at the right time in history to make your body, and your soul chose this time and space and experience to grow and thrive. You've made it here against the odds, and now is the time to start to believe that you are worthy of creating a life that you love. And you are, I promise. I have a very strong intention at the time of writing this that the right people will read it, and if that's you then this message is lining up with that intention. If you have worthiness issues then please find a way to work on them, because they will be affecting everything - money included.

It's time to write your new money story, and attract a different experience. All of the new statements you have made can be formed into powerful affirmations starting with I AM. Read these affirmations to yourself every day and keep searching for and adding in more evidence that you know will support these new empowering money beliefs.

"Someone once said I was deluded,
I nearly fell off my unicorn."

~ Unknown

SELF CARE

"When you work on processing and healing, tough days show up. But always remember that each tough day done, is a day closer to personal freedom."

Emma Eilbeck

Tin Bucket Self Care

If you want to create a life that you love, then you have to be measured in where you "spend" your life force energy. Think of it as a valuable resource, like water.
The Universe gives you a monthly life force energy income, which we can break down into a weekly and daily average amount. You need some of this energy to fuel your regular day to day existence. Take a moment now to consider the energy that you have to spend within the first hour of getting up in the morning. Every task that requires your input is you spending your energy or life force, and that includes thinking and feeling as well as the practical. By the time you've had a shower, made coffee, dressed and left the house you've used up a percentage of your daily life force energy - but this isn't usually as straightforward in the real world.

Add into the mix a text message from an upset friend, a lost sports kit, a child's packed lunch to make, a last minute dash to the shop for bread, the television on in the background with a tragic breaking news story and more....

All of these things pull on our energy and either subtly or not so subtly deplete us of our energy before we even walk out of the door. Then there's the school run followed by the commute followed by finding a parking space and the walk into the office with the colleague that hates their job and their husband. You start to shore up your energy for the 9 to 5 and add in more coffee, which gives you a lift but steals a bit more of your energy as you start to come down in an hour's time. At break time you check your Facebook feed and see that someone has shared the recent news story that you tried to block out this morning, and the tragedy pulls you in again and you feel your energy drop. Whilst you're looking at your phone an email drops in from your kid's school about parents evening. You get a text message from your partner saying that they forgot that they were going out tonight to a meeting, apologies but won't be back in time to take your eldest to football, could you arrange something else. And you remember that you need cat food, milk and fabric conditioner so you make a note to go home via the supermarket, after dropping in to see if your parents need anything - after all they are on the way and you haven't seen them all week. Break time over, you head back into the lion's den and get on with the task at hand, you're so tired and it's only mid-morning.....

Is it any wonder that we end up feeling exhausted and depleted a lot of the time?

Our life force is constantly being sucked out of us in all directions, and in many cases we are so low on it that we don't know it's happening. We avoid looking at how wrung out we feel because we ironically don't have the energy to. But this is the only way that we can stop leaking our life force all over the place. Everyone has busy and stressful times in their life, I get that.

As I sit here and write these words I am nearly 18 months into a house renovation and boy have I felt it. Making decisions, co-ordinating tradesmen and moving furniture from room to room has been exhausting. Not to mention the fact that life cannot be put on hold - I've still had to show up as a parent, a wife, a daughter, a friend and in my work while this was going on, and that has at times left me overdrawn in my own life force account. I've hit the wall a couple of times and had to unplug altogether, handing the day to day running of my business over to colleagues temporarily and letting my friends know I was in lock down. Maybe that's what led me to write this, because I need to learn personally not to take it to the wire before I crash. I have thankfully never had full on burnout, but I have had a wobbly two weeks which I feel were a very close call one summer. So how on earth did this happen and why am I sharing?

Anyone who knows me knows that I am full on here to help other people. Those people might be the people out there in the world that read my books, look for card of the day on my Facebook page or glean something from my blog. If you bring it in a little closer, these are people in my work that connect within the conscious communities and programmes I build or as part of one to one coaching.

Closer still are the group of people that I call friends, and closer again are my family. That's a lot of people and a lot of energy, and you will have a version of this in your life.

But it's good to help so many people, right? It's brave to follow your dream and get out there, isn't it? You need to answer that Calling don't you? Yes, yes and yes. But here's the rub. Where on this list of people do you see me? Absolutely nowhere. And this creates an irony. You end up so energetically overdrawn that you can't give anymore. And you can't show up in the way that you used to. The people I want to be my best for, instead, get a half-arsed diluted version of who I can be, usually grumpy, tired and impatient. That's sad for me and for them. Now I'm not going to go all poor me here, because negative emotions and beating myself up cost even more energy. But what I am going to do is give you an analogy that you can apply to your life moving forwards.

There are two things that you need to do in order to help yourself. One is to stop the life force energy leaking out of you, and the other is to replenish yourself more. Start seeing your life as a tin bucket, and imagine all of the energy drains in your life as holes in this bucket. Some may be bigger than others. Now in your mind's eye fill that bucket with the precious resource of water, which represents the life force energy that we all have flowing through us.

Take a deep breath, close your eyes and connect to yourself. Ask what these holes represent in your life. Are they people, situations, sabotaging behaviours or something different? Where is your energy being drained?

And how can you plug the holes with love and light and an intention to stop the harm to yourself? It's important that you answer this from a self-care perspective, and if you are struggling you can reframe the question like this.

"If I allowed myself to be really honest, who or what would these holes represent?"

Remember that no one else needs to know that you feel this way you are not betraying anyone or being mean. Your focus is the opposite, it is on love and that love is being directed towards yourself. Once you have identified what it is that is draining your energy, you need to make a commitment to bung up the holes and stop your life force energy being so depleted. Ask yourself how you can move away from situations and behaviours that do not serve you. Do you need to stop staying up late and watching negative, drama driven drivel on the television? Do you need to stop spending time at the school gate being part of the gossip machine? Do you need to give up junk food or cut back on alcohol? Do you need to create better boundaries in personal relationships? Do you need to delegate a task or say "no" more often? Ask yourself what would a person who really embraced self-love do if they were in your position right now? Then start to create some action steps for yourself that will help you to make real life actual progress in this direction. Usually the hardest thing for us to do is to disconnect from people in our lives that drain our energy, especially if these are family members or colleagues. It's a much better idea to sidestep these people gradually and gracefully, rather than cutting off the connection suddenly. This is because it's likely to create far less drama, something they may like to thrive on, but equally something that will deplete you even more. Sidestepping can be done by deliberately creating a small amount of distance and better boundaries, and then gradually building on that with the intention that you are freeing you both from a situation that may have become toxic.

Know that if you are not in resonance with someone that they are not in resonance with you either and that this is ultimately right for both of you even if they don't know that at the outset. Once you have practiced plugging up the gaps you are ready to start looking for ways to increase your life force energy. What is it that fills you up? This is different for everyone, but examples could be spending time in nature, reading a novel, a bubble bath, a hobby or a massage. Whatever this is, it doesn't matter - what does matter is how you feel. When you feel good you are going to be topping up your life force energy, and this top up combined with reducing the outflow will mean that you start to feel so much better. And that feeling better will translate into you showing up better for yourself and the people that count, which in turn will make you feel even better and give you back a whole load of self-worth.

Soul Searching Questions

Things or people that deplete my life force energy ~

What action I need to take to stop or reduce this ~

Things that top up my life force energy ~

How I am going to bring more of these into my life ~

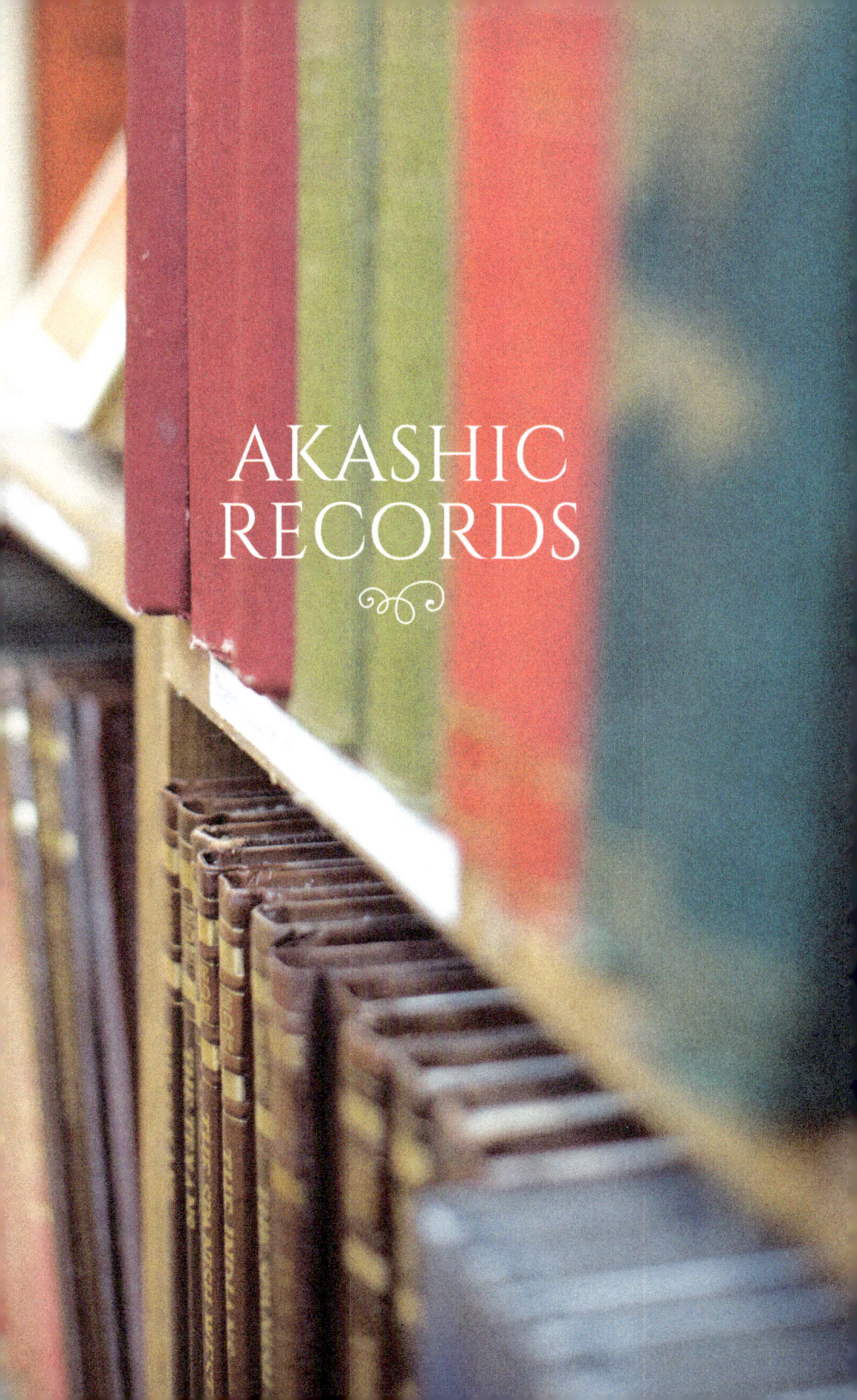

AKASHIC RECORDS

"Whatever's good for your soul - do that."

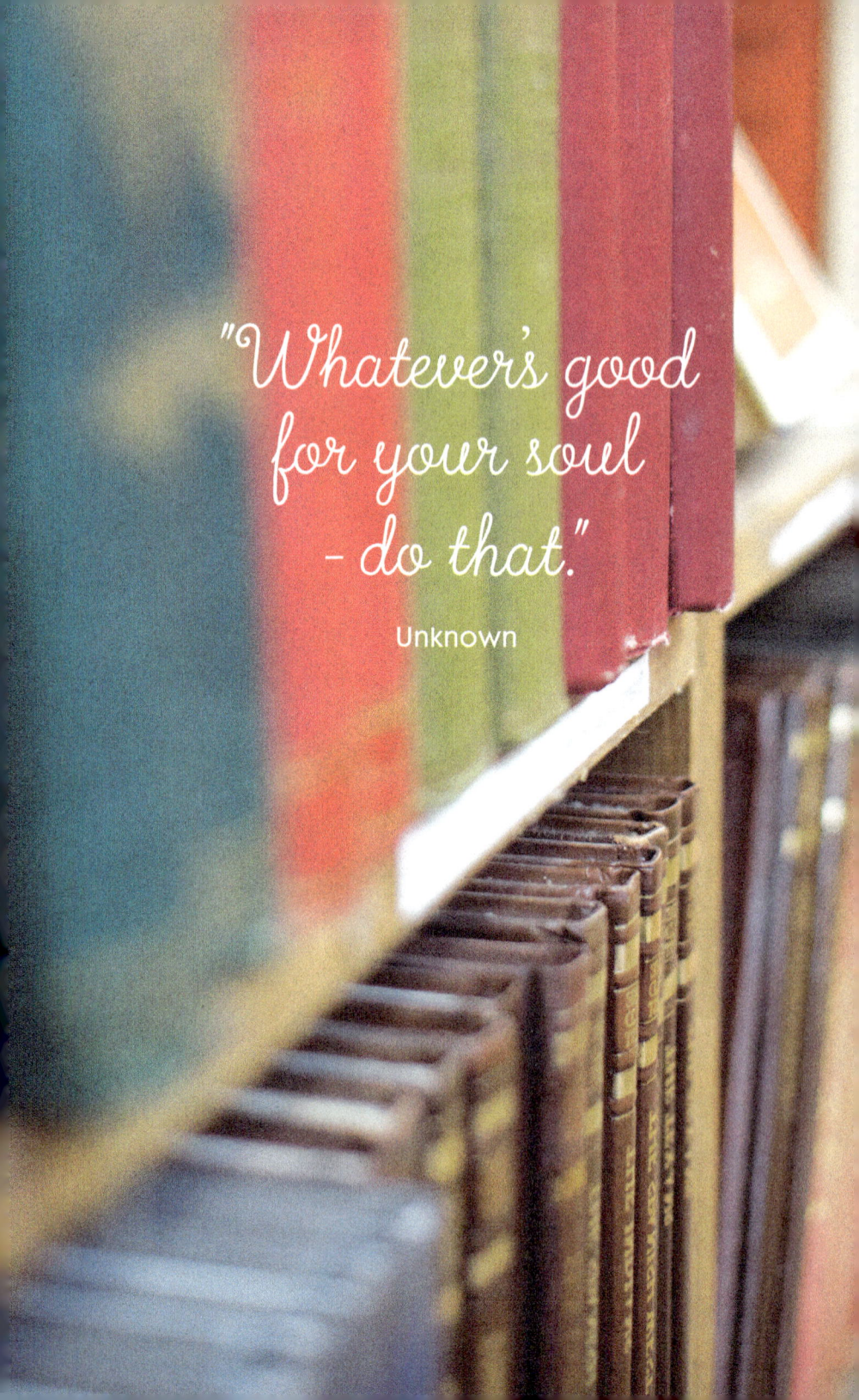

Unknown

Akashic Records

The Akashic Records are a concept that we as a collective have created, to show and represent a "place" where every thought, word, deed and intention is logged by the Universe. In other words every single moment and feeling from every single being in every single lifetime is held there.

You can see why the Akashic Records are also sometimes called The Mind of God, as they are an all-encompassing vibrational account of all that has ever been. As a soul you have your own individual Akashic Record. As humans, the easiest way for us to conceptualise a large amount of data and information all being kept in one place is to consider this a huge archive or library of sorts. This is why we sometimes hear The Hall of Records being referred to as the place that our soul records are held.

Remember that this is a constructed concept for us to be able to get our human thoughts around the idea, and that actually there may not be one fixed place and space that does contain all of this information at the same time. Another name for this cosmic information hub is The Libraries of Light, and some people may have visited them in a quest for answers and insights.

I believe that our human brain creates a framework and idea that we can work with when we are in meditation or under hypnotic regression, a metaphor if you like, that helps us to understand the idea of a lot of information in one place and a piece of this information relating to every soul. This metaphor is what we have called The Akashic Records, and depending on how you process information as an individual and what you believe, you will experience The Akashic Records in a way that fits with you. By using the word "metaphor" I am not saying that this isn't real.

I am saying that this is the best way for our human mind and brain to understand the vastness of information that is out there inter-dimensionally, and that as such we have constructed this concept to help us to try to understand.

My experience of Akashic Records began when I studied to be a Life Between Lives practitioner. Based on the work of Michael Newton, this fascinating method of Soul Regression typically takes a subject back through their most recent past life and into the space "between lives".

Also referred to as the spirit world, or home. I had the amazing experience of visiting "The Library of Light" when in trance, and to me it looked and felt like a big old building with a vast and never ending interior lined with books on several floors. I was aware of other beings around me and when I was asked by my facilitator I said that these were beings that "worked" in the library.

Thoughts were telepathic and I was able to call to one of them to help direct me to my own record. When in trance I saw a large book being brought to me with my name scrolled over the front in gold italics. The book was white and when I opened it, I was able to connect with what looked like moving pictures and images of my life here on earth so far. When I touched an image I was drawn into it as an observer and I could see, feel and hear what was going on in that moment and scenario.

One of the most interesting things was that I could connect with what other people were feeling and thinking, which was very useful in giving me a different perspective on past occurrences. It is probably important to add here that just the same as any other spiritual work, you are going to get what is right for you at this time. If you embark on an Akashic journey, do so with the clear intention that what comes up for you is going to serve you in your life right now.

My soul didn't want to experience any of my past lives, and so they were not brought forwards in my records. Most people that I worked with when I was a practitioner did refer to past lives, and this was always an opportunity to mine for information that may be affecting them in the now in a conscious way with a healing intention.

Common reasons for people wanting to explore their records include why they may have chosen their family, partner or life path. Many of us are also curious about our purpose, calling and reasons for being here. Soul contracts are often brought up in discussion, as well as past life karma, how to heal from pain and trauma and how to create a life they love. And more often than not, people have lost someone close and they simply want to know that there is something else other than this human existence.

Soul Groups

Journeys into the Akashic Records can give you information about your Soul Group. These are the souls who you have incarnated with in this lifetime to help support, learn from and connect with.

Often you have incarnated with them in previous lifetimes (on earth or elsewhere) and you will often find that these are family members and close friends. It is common for members of a Soul Group to have an agreement or a sign so that when you meet up on earth you will know each other. This triggers in us as humans that feeling of familiarity when we meet a stranger, or an instant connection as if you have known someone before.

Often we find that the souls we are closely connected with in this lifetime may have been present in our past lives but had a different role, a parent may now be a child and vice versa. These choices can depend on what we wish to experience during that incarnation and also any lessons that we have agreed to learn for our soul's highest good, or any karma we have to work through.

Typically in a spiritual regression you will become aware of between twelve and fifteen members of your Soul Group, some of these may be people that you have not yet met on the earth plane.

Contracts

These are agreements that are made between souls before they come to earth. Typical Soul Contracts may be an arrangement to meet up and share a certain lesson, period of time or even to experience being together as a couple.

We all come to the earth to learn, grow and experience. Before we arrive in our physical form, it is common to discuss with our guides the lessons and experiences that we want to go through when we get here. These choices include things like our gender, our genetic families, life-changing moments and more.

It is important to mention here that there is a vast amount of information out there on this subject, and as with all of it I encourage you to take what you need. Discernment is important in all aspects of life, but especially subjects like this. Just because something is written down and in print, does not make it true.

Be a truth seeker for yourself, set yourself on a quest to get as much information as you can and then see what feels right to you. I say this because the concept of choosing a body that may be less than perfect, or an earth life that includes hardship and struggle seems ridiculous to our human brain and ego.

I can dress it up as much as the next writer and say that we honour your journey, and that you are reflecting courage to the whole of humanity, but sometimes no matter how you pixie and unicorn it up some people are dealt a shit hand. You need to make sense of what you have been given, and you need to find out what it means to you.

No one has the right to tell you that you "chose" this, or that you had a contract for your ex-husband to treat you badly and then leave you for your best friend.

That said, I encourage you to look at your life from a Higher Self perspective. Step back from the human happenings and the day to day stuff that distracts us all away from the bigger picture of purpose and what it's all about. Get quiet, get into your heart and ask yourself what you came here for and why certain people are in your life, what have you come to teach them and share and vice versa. Call it contracts, luck, destiny or Law of Attraction. I believe that we are in each other's lives for a reason, and finding that out can be an incredible gift to us all.

Past Lives

Personally, I do believe in past lives. That's because I have been regressed and it felt very real to me. Before I'd had that experience I had a healthy curiosity but I wasn't completely sold.

I sometimes still wonder if the brain makes up a metaphor that helps us to piece together information in a tangible way, and we as humans believe this to be a previous incarnation. Let's say that even though I have experienced what I believe to be myself in former lives, that I can still be open minded and consider that this may not be "real", or rather my human and therefore third dimensional concept of real. There is a great deal of evidence from amazing people like Brian Weiss and Michael Newton who have documented thousands of case studies to show that there is something that happens, when we set an intention that we are going to look at our past lives. The interesting thing for me when I met Michael Newton was that although he is a very gentle, spiritual and noble man, he is also a scientist.

He was super clear on not leading a client with questioning and the use of clean language. I feel that this adds a great deal of weight and credence to his work, and I certainly consider him a highly ethical individual to work with. When someone that is as credible as this man gathers up a lot of information that points towards not only the concept of past lives to be valid, but also the between lives existence of souls and energy, then the subject suddenly has a genuine leg to stand on. If you are interested in this subject I highly recommend Michael Newton's books *Journey of Souls* and *Destiny of Souls*.

Future Lives & Experiences

As well as past information it is sometimes possible for you to glean future information and likely possibilities and life paths. This is because your current future is a vibrational match to who you are right now. You are sending out energy in this very moment that is drawing in a whole load of possible outcomes based on your vibration. As you change your thoughts and feelings in your present, you are influencing your vibration which changes likely possible future outcomes. Therefore future possibilities are very fluid and changeable.

You may find when you have access to your records that you can intend and draw in a glimpse or experience of likely future possibilities. These possibilities are showing you what may happen if you stay aligned and continue to release resistance to this outcome. It is important you remember however that these are exactly that - possibilities and not set in stone.

Accessing Your Akashic Records

You can work with a practitioner to access your records. Hypnosis is a frequently used tool for this and can be very helpful in getting you into the super conscious state that you need to connect.

Some people can relax deeply enough by using a guided meditation, and others may want to have their records read by someone here on the earth. This can happen much like a psychic reading or energy reading, and usually an Akashic Reader will want your full name, date and time of birth and they will complete their own journey or meditation into the Halls of Records and ask for your information. They can then channel this into a report for you and may want to email or speak to you in person about what they have found. If they are also a skilled energy worker they may be able to help you in your current life and circumstances by completing any cord cutting or similar things that you need at that time. As with all readings it is important to take what is in resonance with you.

THE POWER OF PEOPLE

"Empathy is the highest form of intelligence."

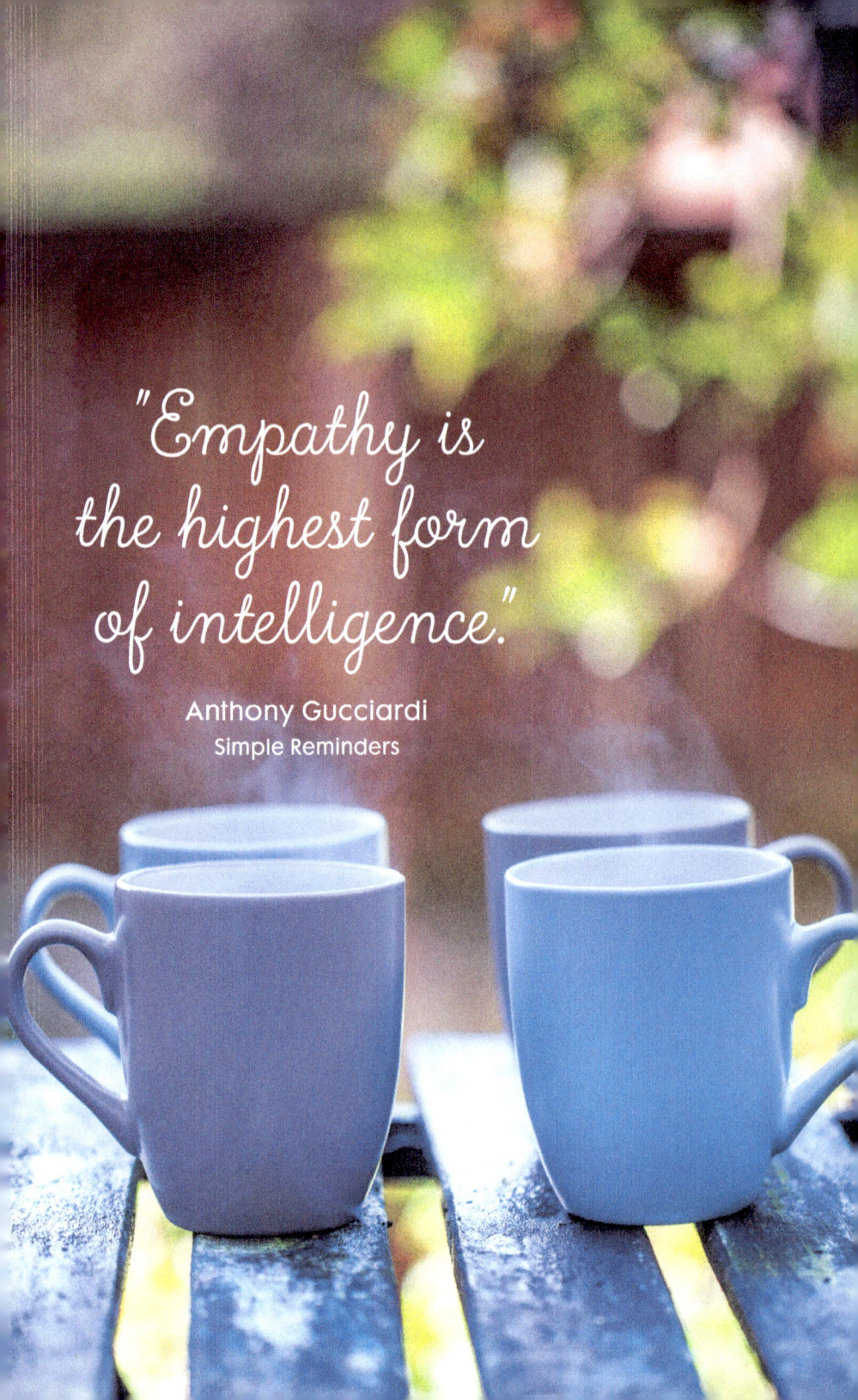

Anthony Gucciardi
Simple Reminders

The Power of People

As you grow, change and evolve, your energy vibration will lift in accordance with your personal and spiritual development. Walking a path of consciousness means your perception of life will widen and shift, and wounds will start to heal. Although this may leave scars on your heart and soul, these become the memories which echo the past, but no longer hold you hostage in a prison of pain.

You strive to raise your standards and the quality of your life and relationships reflect this. Drama is something that is not tolerated or invited, toxic people and situations repel you and anything fake becomes intolerable. The person you are becoming starts to show to others that change is possible, and those entrenched in an old ego story will become defensive.

Law of Attraction starts to happen in reverse, and a kind of energetic dissonance plays out in your life. What used to feel like a good fit for your former lower vibrational self now represents a square peg in a round hole in your life, and you may struggle with friendships, situations and lifestyles that you used to accept and enjoy.

Your light illuminates the aspects of others who are still in the dark, and this can at times make them uncomfortable. Their discomfort and perhaps fear of taking responsibility for their own self sabotage and lack of progress, can drive an ironically false belief that you think you are better than others. This can make the road to living a more conscious and enlightened life a lonely one initially.

As we move away from who and what we no longer feel aligned with, we can find that we enter a gap where we feel quite alone and misunderstood by those close to us. This is when you need to find your Tribe. Seek to surround yourself with people like YOU.

Look for people who lift you up. The dreamers, the action takers and those who believe in miracles. The encouragers, the visionaries and the cheerleaders. The heart centred folks who want to make a difference. Those who want to live consciously, and whom life might have kicked to the kerb but they got back up and learned how to forgive. The people among us who reject cynicism and spite, that live by a strong moral code and have an innate sense of goodness.

As more of us awaken on the planet, the tipping point will occur. And when we gather in numbers there is incredible strength. If you don't have conscious people in your life there are two ways that I know of to connect to more.

The first is my Life & Soul Academy, an online community of like-minded souls that provides member only content and meditations, connection and daily consciousness coaching from me. It's a combination that has changed lives worldwide for many people to date, and provides a safe online haven for life and spiritual evolution. Find out more at www.kate-spencer.com/the-life-soul-academy/.

The second is an innovative online community called The Royal Society formed by the founder of Simple Reminders, Bryant McGill & Jenni Young. It is an online personal development community that breaks down social and cultural barriers whilst helping to nurture thought leaders, build self-worth and confidence. It is a video and member led initiative which holds safe space for you to share and learn in equal measure with a like-minded yet hugely diverse global peer group - you can find out more at Beroyal.com.

Both are worth considering for different reasons and depending on what kind of community your soul is seeking. You may be wondering why am I happy to mention someone else's community alongside my own. Shouldn't I be rounding as many people up into my gang and keeping them for myself?

People who do that are stuck in an old paradigm of fear and control. The vibrational subtext is one of lack, and it's something I have worked hard to get out of. If you can be a stepping stone for someone to connect to other good people, then do it. We need to get out of our self-centred and small-minded human mentality and see the bigger picture here.

We are only going to change the world if we first change ourselves, and that means doing our own work and then showing up as us, knowing that the right people will align with us at the right time for us to serve – whatever that looks like.

We are all in this together. And I don't mind how you wake up and start to live consciously. I just pray that you will.

"Be mindful even if your mind is full."

~ James De La Vega

MINDFULNESS

"Pause and remember –
Every single event in your life,
especially the difficult lessons,
have made you smarter,
stronger, and wiser than you
were yesterday. Be thankful!"

Jenni Young
Simple Reminders

Mindfulness

This is a practice that helps you to not only stay present, but also helps hugely with emotional, mental and physical wellbeing. Practicing mindfulness has been shown to reduce stress, anxiety and depression, and generally make you feel happier and more satisfied in your life. It's free, and it's available to all of us in every single moment, so it's well worth a try to see how it can improve the quality of your life, health and relationships.

The origins of mindfulness are rooted in Buddhism, but as a practice it has become increasingly popular over recent years, as scientific studies have proven its value. Mindfulness has been taught in large corporations to help with productivity, workplace happiness and stress management, and is often recommended by doctors and psychotherapists as part of an overall treatment plan for those that need it. But what exactly is mindfulness?

It's the practice of not only being fully present in a moment, it's about bringing your full awareness and consciousness into that moment. It's a really simple principle that is not simple to master when you are in human form. One of the first things you need to accept is that our mind is an aspect of us, but it's not who we are. Your mind is constantly full of thoughts, and these thoughts are scattered across time, experience, situations, expectations and memories.

You can be doing something in your present moment life, such as washing the dishes - but your mind wanders back to a situation three years ago, or last week, or you hear a text alert on your phone and before you know it your mind is generating a myriad of thoughts that are unrelated to where you are right now. You are suddenly not present but living in the past, the future or a parallel place that isn't the now, on a kind of mental autopilot that takes you away from this exact moment.

Our mind is always going to be presenting us with different thoughts, but it is the process of getting involved in these thoughts that loses mindfulness, presence and consciousness. Observing thoughts without judgment, and not chasing them down the mental rabbit hole that opens up into an endless warren of thought possibilities is the beginning of mindfulness. It is no surprise that mindfulness has been proven to help with our mental health, so many of us spend time wading through negative emotions from the past and then flip to fast forward and live in a place of worry and fear about the future. In the moments when you can be fully mindful, the concept of the past and the future cease to exist and therefore so do their associated feelings. You anchor your consciousness in the now entirely, and therefore that is all there is.

Mindfulness can have a positive effect on your physical wellness. This is because negative or low vibration thoughts (typically guilt, anger, resentment from the past or worry and anxiety about the future) detrimentally affect our physiology. Thoughts create emotions, which in turn create responses in our body, and changes in our cells. Detrimental changes in our physiology and cells creates disease and illness. When you are practicing mindfulness you are not persistently thinking thoughts that are going to generate these emotions, and therefore there is no physical response. In times gone by, this response was useful. If a bear started to run towards us we would generate a fear response in our body that would fuel us to get out of danger or defend ourselves (fight or flight). These days that fear may be generated by thoughts about what might happen next week at work if you don't meet a deadline, or some other human challenge that you are facing. Your body doesn't know that there is no bear, it just knows that your thoughts of worry and anxiety are underpinned by fear, so it triggers the physiological changes that it is wired to create.

The fear reaction in your body brings about changes in your blood pressure, heart rate, cells and more, which can lead to illness and disease as well as further emotional overwhelm and psychological stress. This self-perpetuating cycle can be broken with practicing mindfulness, where you shift your focus back to the present moment and begin to learn to observe and release the thoughts that start the whole thing off. There is no magic switch to turn off your thoughts.

The control that we have however is in the conscious observation of them, non-judgment followed by an intentional release. Mindfulness encourages us to be aware of our thoughts and then gently bring our attention back to an object of focus, this can be your breath, awareness of your body, your immediate environment or something as simple as the colour of the sky that you can see from your window.

In the refocusing of your attention in the now and in a conscious and deliberate way, you can release the thoughts that were going to hook you into moving your energy away from the now, therefore robbing you of concentration, peace and presence. Meditation is a great way to practice mindfulness, and can be done for even just a few minutes at a time to start to gain benefits in health and wellbeing. If you've never tried it, please don't think it's hard or that you need to give up loads of time and sit in a yoga pose for hours. Meditation can simply be you closing your eyes, getting centred and focusing on your breathing for a few moments, or you can try a guided meditation that will take you on a journey and help you to focus your thoughts on what the journey includes instead of intrusive thoughts that you can observe and allow to release. These are especially good to try in the morning to set up your day and before you go to bed in order to get into a peaceful and relaxed state.

Other ways to practice mindfulness can include doing one task at a time and really bringing your entire focus to that task. For example if you are washing dishes in the kitchen sink, feel the temperature of the water, smell the fragrance of the detergent, see the rainbows in the bubbles and feel the contrast of the water that you use to rinse. If your thoughts start to drift from the task at hand, gently bring them back and begin to connect again consciously with what is occurring in that moment.

Mindful eating can be a way of incorporating mindfulness into our lives several times a day and it involves really slowing down and experiencing the food that we are eating in a very conscious way. Being more aware not only of what we are eating and the food choices that we are making, but also of the colour, texture and taste of the food brings a whole new reverence and experience to eating. Sending gratitude to the food on our plate, the source of the food and the Universe can add to this experience.

Deliberate slowing down is another good way to practice mindfulness. This can sound counterproductive especially if you have a lot on your plate, but slowing down can help you to be more present with the task in hand, and can help you with clearer thinking and decision making, therefore saving you time in the longer run. When you find yourself rushing to fit as much in as you can, stop and take a deep breath, bring yourself back in to the present and remind yourself that you can only do as much as you can do and that rushing and putting pressure on yourself is not helping. Take any practical steps you can such as ranking tasks in priority order or delegating, focus on your breathing and regroup for a couple of minutes, knowing that slowing down and being mindful can actually have the effect of speeding things up overall.

A mindful walk can be a great self-care tool. Take yourself off somewhere and as you walk, really notice how you feel, the pressure of the pavement or forest floor beneath your feet, the sounds around you and what you can see. Incorporate all of your senses and allow thoughts to come up, but practice not following them, instead bring your attention back to the now and continue to consciously observe.

Soul Searching Questions

How can I practice being more mindful?

What do I feel I could gain from being more mindful?

What might I be missing out on in my life by not being present?

What can I do when I feel myself not being present?

Goodbye 2017

Closing off the previous year is important. It allows you the mental and emotional space and bandwidth to gain closure on what you need to carry over the learning and the gratitude, and to give yourself permission to start over.

A New Year is the beginning of a new cycle, and in order to embrace all of that lovely positive fresh start vibe, we need to say thank you and goodbye to what has gone before. This does not have to be an outwardly big thing, it can be a personal ritual that tells the Universe that you are ready to step forward into the next part of your journey, with love, grace and New Year Mojo.

Light a candle, burn some incense and get some mood music on if you want to really set the tone. Do this your way, but even if you don't write anything down, give yourself the gift of thinking them through and knowing what your answers would be.

Profound Moments and Experiences ~

Stuff I am Insanely Grateful For ~

What I have learned ~

How I have grown ~

What I take forward with me ~

What I need to leave behind ~

What I need to forgive myself for ~

And so it is.

Hello 2018! My New Story Starts Here

Every month you will have the chance to see what you need to review the month that has passed, work on consciously releasing what you need to, and realigning with what you want to create in your life experience. These moments at the beginning of the month will be really helpful for you, they are the stepping stones that pave the way to your big vision.

Speaking of which, what is it that you want to create this year for yourself?

How do you want your life to look in terms of relationships, health, income, spirituality, joy, happiness, family, career and more? Let's start with getting some of your ideas down on paper so that you can really zone in on what you want to manifest, remember if your mind starts to butt in and give you all kinds of reasons why this stuff can't happen that this is your ego trying to sabotage you (and we all have one!)

Think of it this way, if you had the ability to create everything that you truly desire – what would that look like, sound like, taste like and most importantly feel like. Write Your Story for the coming year in the present tense and create as much detail as you can. The more emotionally charged words and powerful language that you can use, the more feelings you will stir within yourself and the more easily it will be to send then out as a signal for the Universe to match.

Here is an example to get you started….

I am loving the life that I live. Every day is brimming with abundance and health for me, my wellbeing flows so easily these days and I see it manifesting in my experience. I love that fact that I can eat food that nurtures my body and that I can experience a gorgeous hot shower every day. I feel so happy and connected to myself that it is easy to see how the Universe keeps sending me so many opportunities to create more happiness and abundance in my life for me and my family. I can afford to be generous with others and this helps me to stay in fair exchange with all of the goodness I am receiving. I love the simple things in my life like fresh flowers and my garden, which is a metaphor for the way I am growing and evolving. I am surrounded by people that I love, and I feel it in every moment. My life is truly blessed and I know that this year it's just going to get even better. When I feel so blessed I know that the Universe is going to send me even more and this makes me relax into being in the present.

You can put specific goals in your story such as you love having a luxury family holiday, or living in a home that you desire, or driving a car that you want to draw in – but be aware that when you feel really blessed and in the flow that these things come to you as a result of that.

Go ahead – write your big and awesome story for 2018!

Happy New Year
2018

"It's far more important to be perfectly you, than it is to be perfect."

Cat Knott

MY 2018 STORY

HELLO *January*

"I choose to release the past and move forward into the life I am meant for filled with peace, joy, and happiness."

Melissa Zoske

INTENTIONS IN ACTION

I AM *showing myself love this month by:*

....

....

I AM *nurturing relationships this month by:*

....

....

I AM *supporting my physical body this month by:*

....

....

I AM *honouring my spiritual path this month by:*

....

....

I AM *creating abundance for myself this month by:*

....

....

ATTITUDE OF GRATITUDE

This month I AM *in Gratitude for:*

MONTHLY MANIFESTATION

Positive, present moment and personal affirmations...

I AM ....

....

....

I AM ....

....

....

I AM ....

....

....

I AM ....

....

....

I AM ....

....

....

I AM ....

....

....

JANUARY

1 *Monday*   New Year's Day

2 *Tuesday*

3 *Wednesday*

4 *Thursday*

JANUARY

Friday **5**

Saturday **6**

Sunday **7**

JANUARY

8 *Monday*

....

....

....

9 *Tuesday*

....

....

....

10 *Wednesday*

....

....

....

11 *Thursday*

....

....

....

JANUARY

Friday 12

Saturday 13

Sunday 14

JANUARY

15 *Monday*

16 *Tuesday*

17 *Wednesday* ○ New Moon

18 *Thursday*

JANUARY

Friday 19

Saturday 20

Sunday 21

JANUARY

22 *Monday*

23 *Tuesday*

24 *Wednesday*

25 *Thursday*

JANUARY

Friday 26

Burns Night

Saturday 27

Sunday 28

JANUARY/ FEBRUARY

29 *Monday*

30 *Tuesday*

31 *Wednesday* ● **Full Moon**

1 *Thursday*

FEBRUARY

Friday 2

Saturday 3

Sunday 4

THANK YOU JANUARY...
for your lessons, gifts and experiences

REVIEW... *What I learned and what I loved*

....
....
....
....
....

RELEASE... *What I need to forgive and forget*

....
....
....
....
....

RENEW... *What I need to focus on next month*

....
....
....
....
....

NOTES

HELLO *February*

"We can focus on fear or love.
The choice is ours.
We are surrounded by blessings
at every single moment but
we must open our eyes and
hearts to see them."

Anna Grace Taylor

INTENTIONS IN ACTION

I AM *showing myself love this month by:*

....

....

I AM *nurturing relationships this month by:*

....

....

I AM *supporting my physical body this month by:*

....

....

I AM *honouring my spiritual path this month by:*

....

....

I AM *creating abundance for myself this month by:*

....

....

ATTITUDE OF GRATITUDE

This month **I AM** *in Gratitude for:*

MONTHLY MANIFESTATION

Positive, present moment and personal affirmations...

I AM ....

....

....

I AM ....

....

....

I AM ....

....

....

I AM ....

....

....

I AM ....

....

....

I AM ....

....

....

JANUARY/ FEBRUARY

29 Monday

30 Tuesday

31 Wednesday

1 Thursday

FEBRUARY

Friday **2**

Saturday **3**

Sunday **4**

FEBRUARY

5 Monday

6 Tuesday

7 Wednesday

8 Thursday

FEBRUARY

Friday 9

Saturday 10

Sunday 11

FEBRUARY

12 *Monday*

13 *Tuesday*

14 *Wednesday* — Valentine's Day

15 *Thursday* — ◯ New Moon

FEBRUARY

Chinese New Year

Friday **16**

Saturday **17**

Sunday **18**

FEBRUARY

19 *Monday*   U.S.A Holiday - President's Day

20 *Tuesday*

21 *Wednesday*

22 *Thursday*

FEBRUARY

Friday **23**

Saturday **24**

Sunday **25**

FEBRUARY/MARCH

26 Monday

27 Tuesday

28 Wednesday

1 Thursday

MARCH

Friday 2

Saturday 3

Sunday 4

THANK YOU FEBRUARY...
for your lessons, gifts and experiences

REVIEW... *What I learned and what I loved*

RELEASE... *What I need to forgive and forget*

RENEW... *What I need to focus on next month*

NOTES

HELLO *March*

"You are enough means you can grow and change and continue to become, because you aren't trying to prove yourself. You are just trying to be yourself."

Judy McKillop
Surviving Grief

INTENTIONS IN ACTION

I AM showing myself love this month by:

....

....

I AM nurturing relationships this month by:

....

....

I AM supporting my physical body this month by:

....

....

I AM honouring my spiritual path this month by:

....

....

I AM creating abundance for myself this month by:

....

....

ATTITUDE OF GRATITUDE

This month **I AM** *in Gratitude for:*

MONTHLY MANIFESTATION

Positive, present moment and personal affirmations...

I AM

I AM

I AM

I AM

I AM

I AM

FEBRUARY/MARCH

26 Monday

27 Tuesday

28 Wednesday

1 Thursday

MARCH

Full Moon

Friday **2**

Saturday **3**

Sunday **4**

MARCH

5 Monday

6 Tuesday

7 Wednesday

8 Thursday

MARCH

Friday **9**

Saturday **10**

Mother's Day U.K

Sunday **11**

MARCH

12 *Monday*

....

....

....

13 *Tuesday*

....

....

....

14 *Wednesday*

....

....

....

15 *Thursday*

....

....

....

MARCH

Friday 16

Saturday 17

New Moon ○

St Patrick's Day

Sunday 18

MARCH

19 Monday

....
....
....

20 Tuesday

....
....
....

21 Wednesday

....
....
....

22 Thursday   **Mercury Retrograde begins**

....
....
....

MARCH

Friday **23**

Saturday **24**

Sunday **25**

MARCH

26 Monday

27 Tuesday

28 Wednesday

29 Thursday

MARCH/APRIL

Good Friday Friday **30**

Full Moon Saturday **31**

Easter Sunday Sunday **1**

THANK YOU MARCH...
for your lessons, gifts and experiences

REVIEW... *What I learned and what I loved*

RELEASE... *What I need to forgive and forget*

RENEW... *What I need to focus on next month*

NOTES

HELLO
April

"Just because people are unkind to you doesn't mean you have to be unkind back. That's how the world changes - one brave person like you being kind."

Bryant McGill
Simple Reminders

INTENTIONS IN ACTION

I AM *showing myself love this month by:*

....

....

I AM *nurturing relationships this month by:*

....

....

I AM *supporting my physical body this month by:*

....

....

I AM *honouring my spiritual path this month by:*

....

....

I AM *creating abundance for myself this month by:*

....

....

ATTITUDE OF GRATITUDE

This month **I AM** *in Gratitude for:*

MONTHLY MANIFESTATION

Positive, present moment and personal affirmations...

I AM ....

....

....

I AM ....

....

....

I AM ....

....

....

I AM ....

....

....

I AM ....

....

....

I AM ....

....

....

MARCH

26 Monday

27 Tuesday

28 Wednesday

29 Thursday

MARCH/APRIL

Good Friday — Friday **30**

Full Moon — Saturday **31**

Easter Sunday — Sunday **1**

APRIL

2 Monday　　　　　　　　　　　　　　　　　　　　　　　　　　　　　**Easter Monday**

3 Tuesday

4 Wednesday

5 Thursday

APRIL

Friday **6**

Saturday **7**

Sunday **8**

APRIL

9 Monday

10 Tuesday

11 Wednesday

12 Thursday

APRIL

Friday **13**

Saturday **14**

Mercury Retrograde ends *Sunday* **15**

APRIL

16 *Monday* ◯ New Moon

17 *Tuesday*

18 *Wednesday*

19 *Thursday*

APRIL

Friday **20**

Saturday **21**

Sunday **22**

APRIL

23 Monday

24 Tuesday

25 Wednesday

26 Thursday

APRIL

Friday **27**

Saturday **28**

Sunday **29**

THANK YOU APRIL...
for your lessons, gifts and experiences

REVIEW... *What I learned and what I loved*

RELEASE... *What I need to forgive and forget*

RENEW... *What I need to focus on next month*

NOTES

HELLO *May*

"Stillness speaks,
be the quiet presence
that listens."

Brian Thompson
Zen Thinking

INTENTIONS IN ACTION

I AM showing myself love this month by:

....

....

I AM nurturing relationships this month by:

....

....

I AM supporting my physical body this month by:

....

....

I AM honouring my spiritual path this month by:

....

....

I AM creating abundance for myself this month by:

....

....

ATTITUDE OF GRATITUDE

This month **I AM** *in Gratitude for:*

MONTHLY MANIFESTATION

Positive, present moment and personal affirmations...

I AM

I AM

I AM

I AM

I AM

I AM

APRIL/MAY

30 Monday ● Full Moon

1 Tuesday

2 Wednesday

3 Thursday

MAY

Friday **4**

Saturday **5**

Sunday **6**

MAY

7 Monday   U.K Bank Holiday

8 Tuesday

9 Wednesday

10 Thursday

MAY

Friday 11

Saturday 12

Mother's Day U.S.A, Australia & N.Z

Sunday 13

MAY

14 Monday

15 Tuesday ○ New Moon

16 Wednesday

17 Thursday

MAY

Friday 18

Saturday 19

Sunday 20

MAY

21 Monday

22 Tuesday

23 Wednesday

24 Thursday

MAY

Friday **25**

Saturday **26**

Sunday **27**

MAY

28 Monday

U.K Bank Holiday
Memorial Day

29 Tuesday

● Full Moon

30 Wednesday

31 Thursday

JUNE

Friday 1

Saturday 2

Sunday 3

THANK YOU MAY...
for your lessons, gifts and experiences

REVIEW... *What I learned and what I loved*

....
....
....
....
....

RELEASE... *What I need to forgive and forget*

....
....
....
....
....

RENEW... *What I need to focus on next month*

....
....
....
....
....

NOTES

HELLO
June

"I want to meet someone brave enough to love me; brave enough to let down their walls and hold space for us both to flourish."

Heidi Dellaire
Love Wide Open

INTENTIONS IN ACTION

I AM *showing myself love this month by:*

....

....

I AM *nurturing relationships this month by:*

....

....

I AM *supporting my physical body this month by:*

....

....

I AM *honouring my spiritual path this month by:*

....

....

I AM *creating abundance for myself this month by:*

....

....

ATTITUDE OF GRATITUDE

This month **I AM** *in Gratitude for:*

MONTHLY MANIFESTATION

Positive, present moment and personal affirmations...

I AM ....
....
....

I AM ....
....
....

I AM ....
....
....

I AM ....
....
....

I AM ....
....
....

I AM ....
....
....

MAY

28 Monday ... U.K Bank Holiday
Memorial Day

29 Tuesday

30 Wednesday

31 Thursday

JUNE

Friday **1**

Saturday **2**

Sunday **3**

JUNE

4 Monday

---

5 Tuesday

---

6 Wednesday

---

7 Thursday

JUNE

Friday 8

Saturday 9

Sunday 10

JUNE

11 Monday

12 Tuesday

13 Wednesday ◯ New Moon

14 Thursday

JUNE

Friday **15**

Saturday **16**

Father's Day U.K & U.S.A   *Sunday* **17**

JUNE

18 *Monday*

19 *Tuesday*

20 *Wednesday*

21 *Thursday*

JUNE

Friday **22**

Saturday **23**

Sunday **24**

JUNE

25 Monday

26 Tuesday

27 Wednesday

28 Thursday

● Full Moon

JUNE/JULY

Friday **29**

....
....
....

Saturday **30**

....
....
....

Sunday **1**

....
....
....

THANK YOU JUNE...
for your lessons, gifts and experiences

REVIEW... *What I learned and what I loved*

. . . .

. . . .

. . . .

. . . .

. . . .

RELEASE... *What I need to forgive and forget*

. . . .

. . . .

. . . .

. . . .

. . . .

RENEW... *What I need to focus on next month*

. . . .

. . . .

. . . .

. . . .

. . . .

NOTES

HELLO
July

"Accept the apology you'll never receive."

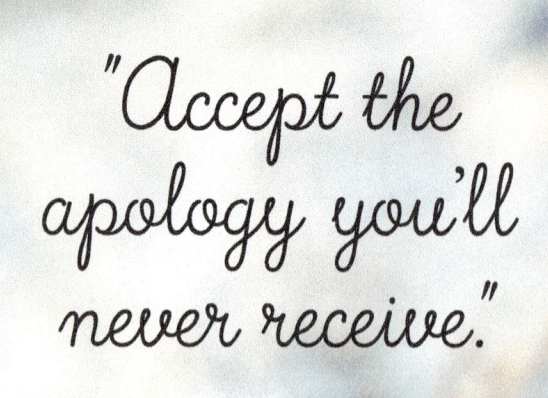

Dr. Shawne Duperon
Project Forgive

INTENTIONS IN ACTION

I AM *showing myself love this month by:*

....

....

I AM *nurturing relationships this month by:*

....

....

I AM *supporting my physical body this month by:*

....

....

I AM *honouring my spiritual path this month by:*

....

....

I AM *creating abundance for myself this month by:*

....

....

ATTITUDE OF GRATITUDE

This month **I AM** *in Gratitude for:*

MONTHLY MANIFESTATION

Positive, present moment and personal affirmations...

I AM..
....

I AM..
....

I AM..
....

I AM..
....

I AM..
....

I AM..
....

JUNE

25 Monday

26 Tuesday

27 Wednesday

28 Thursday ● Full Moon

JUNE/JULY

Friday 29

Saturday 30

Sunday 1

JULY

2 *Monday*

....
....
....

3 *Tuesday*

....
....
....

4 *Wednesday*   **U.S.A Holiday - Independence Day**

....
....
....

5 *Thursday*

....
....
....

JULY

Friday **6**

Saturday **7**

Sunday **8**

JULY

9 *Monday*

10 *Tuesday*

11 *Wednesday*

12 *Thursday*

JULY

New Moon ○

Friday **13**

Saturday **14**

Sunday **15**

JULY

16 *Monday*

....
....
....

17 *Tuesday*

....
....
....

18 *Wednesday*

....
....
....

19 *Thursday*

....
....
....

JULY

Friday 20

Saturday 21

Sunday 22

JULY

23 Monday

24 Tuesday

25 Wednesday

26 Thursday **Mercury Retrograde begins**

JULY

Full Moon ●

Friday **27**

Saturday **28**

Sunday **29**

JULY/AUGUST

30 Monday

31 Tuesday

1 Wednesday

2 Thursday

AUGUST

Friday 3

Saturday 4

Sunday 5

THANK YOU JULY...
for your lessons, gifts and experiences

REVIEW... *What I learned and what I loved*

RELEASE... *What I need to forgive and forget*

RENEW... *What I need to focus on next month*

NOTES

HELLO August

"The heart can hear what words can't speak."

Holly Kellums
Simple Reminders

INTENTIONS IN ACTION

I AM *showing myself love this month by:*

....

....

I AM *nurturing relationships this month by:*

....

....

I AM *supporting my physical body this month by:*

....

....

I AM *honouring my spiritual path this month by:*

....

....

I AM *creating abundance for myself this month by:*

....

....

ATTITUDE OF GRATITUDE

This month **I AM** *in Gratitude for:*

MONTHLY MANIFESTATION

Positive, present moment and personal affirmations...

I AM ....

....

....

I AM ....

....

....

I AM ....

....

....

I AM ....

....

....

I AM ....

....

....

I AM ....

....

....

JULY/AUGUST

30 Monday

31 Tuesday

1 Wednesday

2 Thursday

AUGUST

Friday **3**

Saturday **4**

Sunday **5**

AUGUST

6 Monday

7 Tuesday

8 Wednesday

9 Thursday

AUGUST

Friday 10

Saturday 11

New Moon ○

Sunday 12

AUGUST

13 *Monday*

14 *Tuesday*

15 *Wednesday*

16 *Thursday*

AUGUST

Friday 17

Mercury Retrograde ends

Saturday 18

Sunday 19

AUGUST

20 *Monday*

21 *Tuesday*

22 *Wednesday*

23 *Thursday*

AUGUST

Friday **24**

Saturday **25**

Full Moon ●　　　　　　　　　　　　　　　　　　　　　　*Sunday* **26**

AUGUST

27 Monday   U.K Bank Holiday

....

....

....

28 Tuesday

....

....

....

29 Wednesday

....

....

....

30 Thursday

....

....

....

AUGUST/SEPTEMBER

Friday **31**

Saturday **1**

Sunday **2**

THANK YOU AUGUST...
for your lessons, gifts and experiences

REVIEW... *What I learned and what I loved*

RELEASE... *What I need to forgive and forget*

RENEW... *What I need to focus on next month*

NOTES

HELLO
September

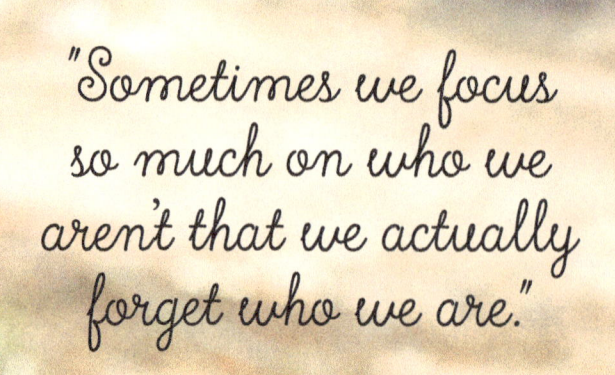

"Sometimes we focus so much on who we aren't that we actually forget who we are."

Aimee Halpin

INTENTIONS IN ACTION

I AM *showing myself love this month by:*

....

....

I AM *nurturing relationships this month by:*

....

....

I AM *supporting my physical body this month by:*

....

....

I AM *honouring my spiritual path this month by:*

....

....

I AM *creating abundance for myself this month by:*

....

....

ATTITUDE OF GRATITUDE

This month **I AM** *in Gratitude for:*

MONTHLY MANIFESTATION

Positive, present moment and personal affirmations...

I AM ....
....
....

I AM ....
....
....

I AM ....
....
....

I AM ....
....
....

I AM ....
....
....

I AM ....
....
....

AUGUST

27 Monday   U.K Bank Holiday

28 Tuesday

29 Wednesday

30 Thursday

AUGUST/SEPTEMBER

Friday **31**

Saturday **1**

Sunday **2**

SEPTEMBER

3 Monday   U.S.A Holiday - Labor Day

4 Tuesday

5 Wednesday

6 Thursday

SEPTEMBER

Friday **7**

Saturday **8**

New Moon ○   *Sunday* **9**

SEPTEMBER

10 *Monday*

11 *Tuesday*

12 *Wednesday*

13 *Thursday*

SEPTEMBER

Friday **14**

Saturday **15**

Sunday **16**

SEPTEMBER

17 *Monday*

18 *Tuesday*

19 *Wednesday*

20 *Thursday*

SEPTEMBER

Friday 21

Saturday 22

Sunday 23

SEPTEMBER

24 *Monday*

25 *Tuesday* ● Full Moon

26 *Wednesday*

27 *Thursday*

SEPTEMBER

Friday **28**

Saturday **29**

Sunday **30**

THANK YOU SEPTEMBER...

for your lessons, gifts and experiences

REVIEW... *What I learned and what I loved*

....
....
....
....
....

RELEASE... *What I need to forgive and forget*

....
....
....
....
....

RENEW... *What I need to focus on next month*

....
....
....
....
....

NOTES

HELLO
October

"When life appears to be working against you, look within. As within, so without."

Trudy Brookes
Awakening Touch

INTENTIONS IN ACTION

I AM *showing myself love this month by:*

....

....

I AM *nurturing relationships this month by:*

....

....

I AM *supporting my physical body this month by:*

....

....

I AM *honouring my spiritual path this month by:*

....

....

I AM *creating abundance for myself this month by:*

....

....

ATTITUDE OF GRATITUDE

This month **I AM** *in Gratitude for:*

MONTHLY MANIFESTATION

Positive, present moment and personal affirmations...

I AM ....
....
....

I AM ....
....
....

I AM ....
....
....

I AM ....
....
....

I AM ....
....
....

I AM ....
....
....

OCTOBER

1 *Monday*

2 *Tuesday*

3 *Wednesday*

4 *Thursday*

OCTOBER

Friday **5**

Saturday **6**

Sunday **7**

OCTOBER

8 Monday   U.S.A Holiday (some States) - Columbus Day

9 Tuesday   ◯ New Moon

10 Wednesday

11 Thursday

OCTOBER

Friday 12

Saturday 13

Sunday 14

OCTOBER

15 *Monday*

16 *Tuesday*

17 *Wednesday*

18 *Thursday*

OCTOBER

Friday 19

Saturday 20

Sunday 21

OCTOBER

22 *Monday*

23 *Tuesday*

24 *Wednesday* 🟣 **Full Moon**

25 *Thursday*

OCTOBER

Friday 26

Saturday 27

Sunday 28

OCTOBER/NOVEMBER

29 *Monday*

30 *Tuesday*

31 *Wednesday*   **Halloween**

1 *Thursday*

NOVEMBER

Friday 2

Saturday 3

Sunday 4

THANK YOU OCTOBER...
for your lessons, gifts and experiences

REVIEW... *What I learned and what I loved*

RELEASE... *What I need to forgive and forget*

RENEW... *What I need to focus on next month*

NOTES

HELLO
November

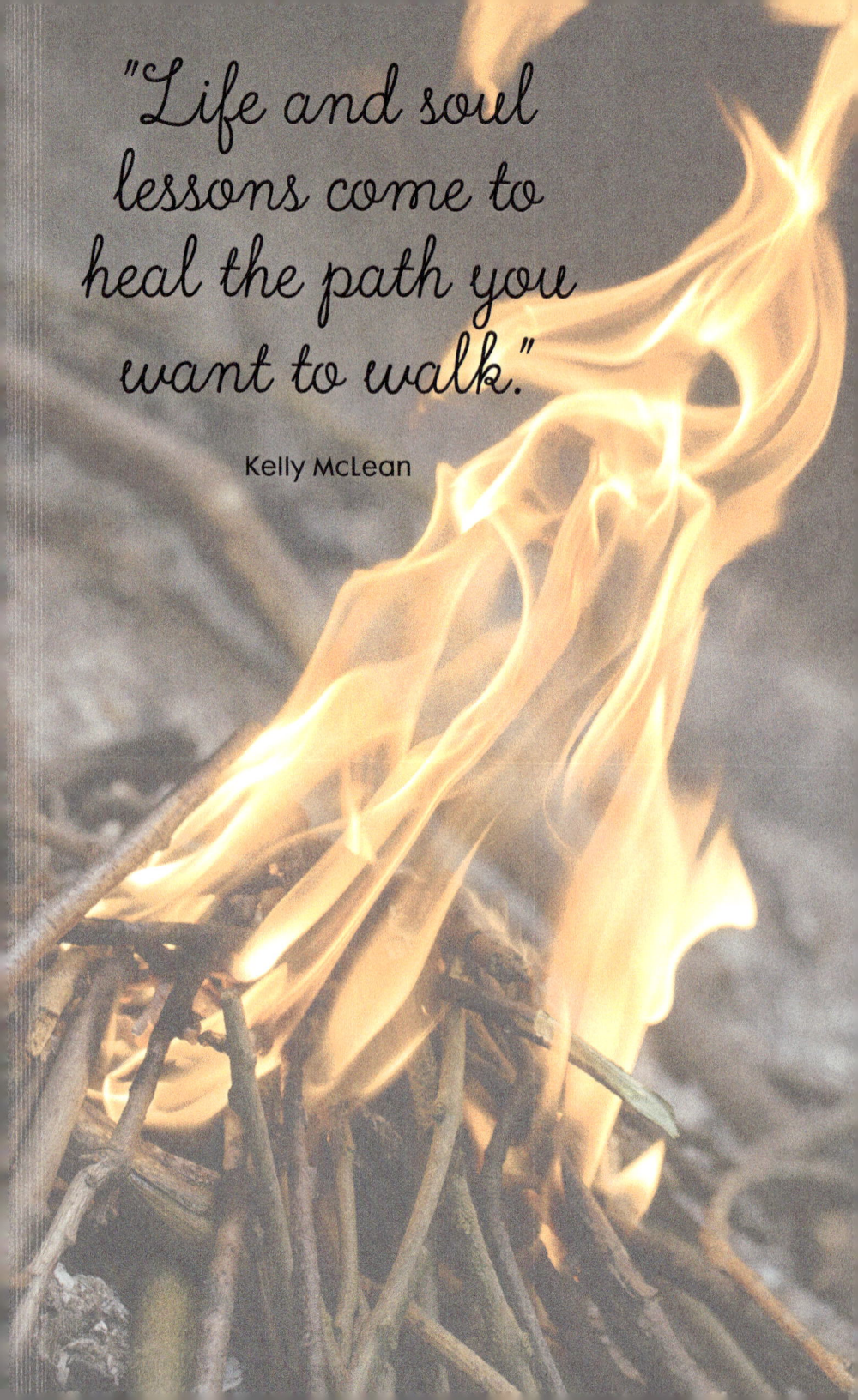

"Life and soul lessons come to heal the path you want to walk."

Kelly McLean

INTENTIONS IN ACTION

I AM *showing myself love this month by:*

....

....

I AM *nurturing relationships this month by:*

....

....

I AM *supporting my physical body this month by:*

....

....

I AM *honouring my spiritual path this month by:*

....

....

I AM *creating abundance for myself this month by:*

....

....

ATTITUDE OF GRATITUDE

This month **I AM** *in Gratitude for:*

MONTHLY MANIFESTATION

Positive, present moment and personal affirmations...

I AM ....

....

....

I AM ....

....

....

I AM ....

....

....

I AM ....

....

....

I AM ....

....

....

I AM ....

....

....

OCTOBER/NOVEMBER

29 Monday

30 Tuesday

31 Wednesday					Halloween

1 Thursday

NOVEMBER

Friday **2**

Saturday **3**

Sunday **4**

NOVEMBER

5 Monday

6 Tuesday

7 Wednesday ◯ New Moon

8 Thursday

NOVEMBER

Friday **9**

....
....
....

Saturday **10**

....
....
....

U.S.A Holiday - Veteran's Day   *Sunday* **11**

....
....
....

NOVEMBER

12 *Monday*

13 *Tuesday*

14 *Wednesday*

15 *Thursday*

NOVEMBER

Mercury Retrograde begins

Friday **16**

Saturday **17**

Sunday **18**

NOVEMBER

19 Monday

20 Tuesday

21 Wednesday

22 Thursday U.S.A Holiday - Thanksgiving Day

NOVEMBER

Full Moon ●

Friday **23**

Saturday **24**

Sunday **25**

NOVEMBER

26 Monday

27 Tuesday

28 Wednesday

29 Thursday

NOVEMBER/DECEMBER

Friday **30**

Saturday **1**

Sunday **2**

THANK YOU NOVEMBER...
for your lessons, gifts and experiences

REVIEW... *What I learned and what I loved*

....

....

....

....

....

RELEASE... *What I need to forgive and forget*

....

....

....

....

....

RENEW... *What I need to focus on next month*

....

....

....

....

....

NOTES

HELLO December

"Sometimes a little rain is necessary to lift the fog."

Sherry Gunn

INTENTIONS IN ACTION

I AM showing myself love this month by:

....

....

I AM nurturing relationships this month by:

....

....

I AM supporting my physical body this month by:

....

....

I AM honouring my spiritual path this month by:

....

....

I AM creating abundance for myself this month by:

....

....

ATTITUDE OF GRATITUDE

This month **I AM** *in Gratitude for:*

MONTHLY MANIFESTATION

Positive, present moment and personal affirmations...

I AM ....

....

....

I AM ....

....

....

I AM ....

....

....

I AM ....

....

....

I AM ....

....

....

I AM ....

....

....

NOVEMBER

27 Monday

28 Tuesday

29 Wednesday

30 Thursday

NOVEMBER/DECEMBER

Friday **30**

Saturday **1**

Sunday **2**

DECEMBER

3 *Monday*

4 *Tuesday*

5 *Wednesday*

6 *Thursday* — **Mercury Retrograde ends**

DECEMBER

New Moon ○

Friday **7**

Saturday **8**

Sunday **9**

DECEMBER

10 Monday

11 Tuesday

12 Wednesday

13 Thursday

DECEMBER

Friday **14**

Saturday **15**

Sunday **16**

DECEMBER

17 *Monday*

18 *Tuesday*

19 *Wednesday*

20 *Thursday*

DECEMBER

Friday 21

Full Moon

Saturday **22**

Sunday **23**

DECEMBER

24 *Monday*   Christmas Eve

25 *Tuesday*   Christmas Day

26 *Wednesday*   Boxing Day

27 *Thursday*

DECEMBER

Friday **28**

Saturday **29**

Sunday **30**

DECEMBER/JANUARY

31 *Monday*   **New Year's Eve**

1 *Tuesday*   **New Year's Day**

2 *Wednesday*

3 *Thursday*

JANUARY

Friday 4

Saturday 5

New Moon ◯   Sunday 6

THANK YOU DECEMBER...
for your lessons, gifts and experiences

REVIEW... *What I learned and what I loved*

RELEASE... *What I need to forgive and forget*

RENEW... *What I need to focus on next month*

"Endings are really just new beginnings."

~ Love Kate x

Goodbye and THANK YOU 2018

HELLO 2019 *I welcome you with an open heart*

"Don't be afraid to walk your own path, the route less travelled has the most beautiful view."

Emma Holmes
Rebels & Rockstars

Acknowledgements

A BIG thank you to my design team...

Michelle Emerson, content edit & typeset
~ www.thewritersassistant.co.uk

Leanne Kelly, diary & graphic design
~ www.facebook.com/Jakenna.creative.design

Simon Avery, cover design
~ www.idobookcovers.com

Photography by Sarah Loveland
~ www.sarahloveland.com

www.kate-spencer.com

My gift to you...
Download your Twelve Lessons Journal audio mp3s here:
www.kate-spencer.com/twelve-lessons-journal-2018-bonuses/

Lightning Source UK Ltd.
Milton Keynes UK
UKOW07f0939261117
313281UK00009BA/180/P